New Orleans

SEAFOOD
COOKBOOK

New Orleans SEAFOOD COOKBOOK

Andrew Jaeger *with* John DeMers

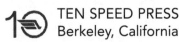
TEN SPEED PRESS
Berkeley, California

Ten Speed Press
P.O. Box 7123
Berkeley, California 94707
www.tenspeed.com

Distributed in Australia by Simon and Schuster Australia, in Canada by Ten Speed Press Canada, in New Zealand by Southern Publishers Group, in South Africa by Real Books, in Southeast Asia by Berkeley Books, and in the United Kingdom and Europe by Airlift Books.

Design by Toni Tajima
Photography by Michael Palumbo

Library of Congress Cataloging-in-Publication Data
on file with publisher

First printing, 1999
Printed in the United States of America

1 2 3 4 5 6 7 8 9 10 — 03 02 01 00 99

CONTENTS

ACKNOWLEDGMENTS

FIRST of all, I would like to thank my father, Charles Jaeger, for showing me the restaurant business and giving me the experience to prosper in it, and my mother, Mary Jaeger, for helping me realize the joy of preparing food for others. I thank my mother's sister, Joy Lynn Cure, and our great family cook, Ruth Joseph, for their history of food and family—particularly their tales of the early days of the Jaeger restaurant. I thank my rock-solid brother Allen for lending his support, facility, and vast knowledge of seafood. I thank Captain John Jurisich for teaching me the oyster business and arranging our trip into oyster country with our great guide Kirt Guerra. I thank the Sunseris—Al, Sal, and Mary—of P & J Oysters, Lenny Minutillo of Louisiana Seafood Exchange, Captain Sammy Slavich, and Captain Frank Moore for the photo ops.

Words of thanks and praise are hardly enough for chef Don James as a mentor, a strong right hand, and a friend of undying loyalty. Chef Don has stuck by me through this project and a thousand others. Thank you, John DeMers, for showing me the way. Last but not least, I thank my soulmate, Rhoda Yawn, and our children, Genevieve and Lauren, for making a home for me and putting up with all my moods and ideas. I love you all!

INTRODUCTION

I grew up in the physical heart and emotional soul of New Orleans. I figured everybody lived as we Jaegers did, in rooms above what, for forty-five years, was the city's most famous seafood house. Every child, I imagined, gazed out from a playpen behind a bar, just short of being able to grab a beer. Every infant, I figured, had a flourish of waitresses rushing to hug, bounce, or tickle him between courses of filé gumbo, shrimp Creole, and redfish court bouillon. And every infant came of age bumping along bayou roads in search of oysters, crawfish, or trout, learning from his daddy that if you buy something for one price and sell it for more, you have the makings of a future in this world.

I learned from my mother, too, as she balanced my father's German hustle with Sicilian passion and religion. Both of these traits were essential to New Orleans food, since everybody here of every race, denomination, or social standing embraced cooking as life's deepest meaning. And everybody lived by the Catholic calendar, with that saga of repentance and renewal that gave New Orleans both Lent and Mardi Gras. I learned at a very young age that in New Orleans, everything didn't have to be a party as long as it came before or after one.

My father's restaurant, called simply "Jaeger's Seafood Tavern," was my playground when I was growing up. There, beginning in what was barely a bar but growing into a complex covering two city blocks on the

The original Jaeger's Restaurant, 1963

broad avenue named Elysian Fields, I ran and jumped and laughed and stumbled, always within sight, scent, and touch of fresh seafood.

The fact that these many years later my French Quarter restaurants specialize in seafood should come as no surprise. And now I'm big enough to grab a beer.

This is our story. It's one story, and yet it's many stories, all fed by seafood in more ways than one. You see, the roads that led my dad, my brother Allen, and me into the marshes to buy product also carried us into the handshakes, backslaps, and grins from a thousand people who lived off the water. These people aspired to no corporate promotions, deserved no awards for fashion or grooming, and usually didn't speak English too well. But they were my world.

That world was slower than things tend to be now, more dependent on season, weather, and luck. We made our trips into rustic Louisiana with my father's employees, his relatives by blood or marriage, and his gambling and drinking buddies. (And usually, it was hard to tell which was which.)

No one in my family ever told me exactly why the first Jaeger came to the New World from Alsace-Lorraine, but it's a safe bet it was a lot like the lures that brought a million others: bigger, better, faster, more. All I know is that by 1820 there were Jaegers doing business here in New Orleans.

Allen and Andrew Jaeger, ages 4 and 3 years

Two things were clear from the start, at least whatever start we know about. One was that "Charles" and "Andrew" were the magic names in our family. Son followed father followed grandfather with one of those names, meaning that when my family gets going with its memories, it's hard to tell which Charles or Andrew they're talking about. The other thing we see is that two professions, or at least two addictive vocations, would reach out and grab Jaeger men: food and music. The fact that I've hardly ever had a restaurant without live music is my way of being true to my roots.

The first Charles Jaeger was a musician who played in a band during the Civil War. After that sad period and the sadder one that followed, Charles and a partner opened a conservatory on St. Charles

Avenue. Charles Jaeger had a son, and the partner, named Messer-schmidt, had a daughter. Those two kids got married, quickly produced my grandfather, and before long, they and a whole bunch of relatives were running a restaurant in tiny Natchez Alley. To the best of our knowledge, the place specialized in deer, bear, and other game.

None of this should obscure the fact that during this time, the 1880s and 1890s, the real hero of our family was Cedric Jaeger. Cedric was a jazz drummer, and quite a great one, it seems. I didn't know much about him until a German man dining in my House of Seafood asked if I was related to the famous jazz drummer. Sometimes, you have to leave it to Europeans to know our music (and sometimes even our relatives!) better than we do.

My older brothers Mike and Charles at the restaurant, 1955

My grandfather Andrew and his brother Charles only dabbled in the restaurant business, but my father (named Charles, but mostly called Charley) jumped in with both feet, beginning in 1936. Before long, my mother was cooking and perfecting recipes. Once we were old enough to walk, my brother Allen and I were running the front of the house. Well, at least we were there, and we were usually running.

To be precise, my father's first efforts were more bars than restaurants. Some people, probably those sharing our German heritage, called these small neighborhood "beergardens." My favorite story about these early days concerns the time my father visited local breweries, hoping they would spring for a free sign, as they did for so many bars. He ended up talking with the folks at Dixie, the kingpin among local breweries. Instead of a sign, he got a warning.

"Listen, Charley," they told my dad, "you can't make it here. There are forty-eight other bars in the same neighborhood."

For the rest of his years in business, my father boasted that every one of those places was long gone, and his business was thriving.

The move from drinking to eating at Jaeger's had a lot to do with my mother. My dad, I think, could have run a bar forever, especially since it was the perfect way to drink and tell stories and to gamble on anything that walked, swam, crawled, or galloped. It was my mother, with her Catholic upbringing, who took the twice-before-married Charley Jaeger and steered him toward something more wholesome. If my mother was sacred, as I like to think, my dad was as profane as they come. They made quite a team.

My mother refused to work behind a bar, but she seemed happy enough over a stove. And that's where she was in the early days of Jaeger's, joined eventually by a host of Creole cooks known to me as Miz Mildred, Xenobia, Annie Roo, and other colorful names. Mama cooked everything Sicilian, which is enough to keep most diners happy. But the Creoles brought along their gumbos, sauce piquants, and court bouillons, and their seasonings for boiling and frying seafood. My mother didn't understand or approve of every trick they pulled in the pan. But whenever the customers loved the food, Mother was smart enough to let the cooks have their way.

That seafood they cooked pointed my father in the direction of what he did best—better, in fact, than anybody I've ever known. He

Mary Jaeger, age 30

was a seafood buyer with a serious case of smarts. He knew what was good, what was fresh, how to get it almost anytime or anywhere, and he knew how to buy and sell it at a profit. Other restaurant people start their day making stocks and sauces, or perhaps counting forks, knives, and napkins. My father figured any relative or friend of the family could be paid to do that. He was in his truck, grinding and slipping down muddy bayou roads through parishes with names like Plaquemines and St. Bernard, to villages with names like Hopedale and Cocodrie, Des Allemands and Delacroix.

My dad would drag along crawfish traps (and usually Allen and me to do the work) and catch forty or fifty pounds in the swamp. He'd hear about some guy who had a bunch of blue crabs or some sacks of fat, salty oysters, or three hampers of perfect softshells, and he'd make a stop there too. Before we knew it, the truck was full. Allen and I were exhausted (if you haven't worked stacking oysters on a flatbed, you haven't really worked!), and the dinner crowd was waiting on Elysian Fields.

On the way back to Jaeger's, Dad would stop at some mom-and-pop eateries, sell them enough seafood to get them going, and take the best stuff back to our place. At some point in each trip, for more than half a century, my dad knew it was nothing but profit ("gravy," as we say in New Orleans) from there.

Charles Jaeger, Uncle George Nasello, and a Jax Beer salesman, 1961

When I look back at my dad's time, which predated the strangling legalities of today's restaurant business, I sometimes feel jealous. These days you can't wipe a pot without a permit, or maybe calling in an Inspector of Pot Wiping—at a healthy fee, of course. My father didn't have to deal with any of that. But what really gets to me is the different way he collected employees.

Today, we hire people based on their training or experience. When my dad hired somebody, it was for one reason alone—the person needed a job. As a result of such unforced charity, Jaeger's became a sanctuary for men who'd gotten behind in their debts (New Orleans had people with whom this was a very dangerous idea), women whose husbands had died or disappeared, teenage cousins who just might be saved from the penitentiary. A lot of these people were related to our family, regardless of how light or dark their skin. Some of my closest aunts and uncles weren't related by blood at all. They simply knew that my father had a restaurant, that he had made some money, and that he could be counted on to help.

Charles Jaeger and friends, 1936

Sometimes, when I was working overtime to make my father the villain of this piece, something would happen to remind me of the spell he cast on people. For instance, there was the time a successful New Orleans lawyer took me to my first dinner at Antoine's.

There I was, more dressed up than I ever like to be, wondering whether I even knew how to act in such a palace. The trick at Antoine's, I'd heard all my life, was having your own waiter, someone who could squeeze you in when they were booked and get you all the best stuff from the kitchen. I figured, as outsiders often do about insiders, that this lawyer had Antoine's locked.

Andrew, Allen, Mary, and Charley Jaeger

Well, we walk in the door, and the first person I see is Numa, one of our regular customers. Numa turns out to be one of Antoine's two senior waiters, the kind bank presidents wait years to inherit. "Hey, Andrew!" he shouts from across the room. "How's your daddy and mama?" This being New Orleans, Numa insisted upon being our waiter. It turns out this lawyer had been trying to get Numa for years.

Other times, it was just the mystery of it all that appealed to me. I don't mean the mystery of crawfish or shrimp or oysters, but of just serving customers. You know them for years, every Friday, every Monday, whatever; you watch their parents grow old, their children grow up, and yet you never really know them at all.

There was one Sicilian guy who used to come in every Sunday morning, at maybe eleven o'clock, when we weren't quite ready to open for lunch. Of course, we let him in, because we all knew him. This guy was perfectly dressed, in a shiny, expensive suit, and his hair was always slicked back perfectly. So I, a kid at the time, would ask him every Sunday why he was so dressed up.

"Andrew," he'd say in a gravely voice, sipping some coffee or maybe something with a kick, "I just come from church." That was it, for all those years: "I just come from church."

When I grew up, I discovered this man in the perfect suit with the perfect haircut ran all the nightclubs on Bourbon Street. He wasn't going out for Sunday morning, he was heading home from Saturday night. It's a safe bet church didn't figure in much of anywhere.

When I was getting serious about the restaurant business, I decided that my father's ideas, habits, and entire attitude were just too old-fashioned. I would implement a new way of running a restaurant, and I would begin by conducting a customer survey. Oh, I knew what my father would say about such things—of course, I can't print what he actually said. But I was convinced the only way we could take care of customers was by knowing as much as we could about them.

My questions were simple and direct, especially the one that asked, "Why do you come to eat at Jaeger's?" I distributed my survey and waited for science, like the saints, to come marching in. What marched in wasn't science. What marched in I'm not even sure what to call.

"I eat at Jaeger's," a regular customer wrote, "because years and years ago, Charley Jaeger helped me when I was in a crisis. He didn't know me then, and he doesn't know me now. But I'll eat at Jaeger's till the day I die."

By 1979, I had had it with trying to do things my way within the confines of having to do them my dad's way. Sure, the big things were working, the food and service, the runs along the bayou for seafood, and certainly the money. But everything seemed such a battle. Eventually, I had done so much around Jaeger's I felt I had more to offer than I was allowed to contribute. I wanted to change things to make them work better. My dad argued that things mustn't be changed, that they were working well enough. As usual, both sides had valid points. But it didn't help me feel any less restless.

I decided to open my own place, in suburban Metairie, where much of the population seemed to be heading. Many of our customers were driving from Metairie by this time, as our neighborhood changed.

The first of my restaurants, Andrew Jaeger's Seafood, was an instant hit. I'm sure it was 1 percent my savvy and 99 percent my family name, but who's counting? It had never occurred to me to play chef, or even to spend time in the kitchen. But I had hired a legend to make my food happen. Joe Martin was the same kind of homegrown, no-nonsense genius that used to cook beside my mother, a true master of Creole cooking.

I was making money. Back then (as now, and sometimes unfortunately), I'd get excited about some new idea, style of cooking, or space that was available, and I'd just have to try my hand. Talk about never resting on your laurels—I never rested! Before the oil bust of 1985 dragged me and a whole bunch of other folks down, Andrew Jaeger's had expanded.

Believe me, these weren't just spinoffs but new—and sometimes bizarre—concepts. At least one, called Andy's Fish Grill, might have worked if I'd waited a few years past 1983, when grilled fish was suddenly everybody's passion. Others were just, for me, stops along the railroad tracks: a breakfast place called Magnolia Grill, Jaeger's Seafood Beergarden at the Lakefront (which still does well for my brother), Andrew Jaeger's Catfish House. . . . Sometimes when I look back at each of these eighteen or twenty restaurants, I wonder what I must have been drinking at the time.

When I came to the French Quarter in 1993, I was about ready for basket weaving. Bankruptcy had taken its toll, even if it had pushed me into the kitchen for both survival and therapy. As it turned out, cooking was great for both.

Mary, Charley, and Andrew at Andrew's first restaurant, about 1980

I opened Andrew Jaeger's House of Seafood (the name, for me, summarized New Orleans and my life) in 1993. It was just a fifty-seat place, and I was the only cook. I wanted live music, so I hired live musicians, even though there was no way fifty seats were going to pay for them. It was just me; nobody could tell me what not to do.

By the time that location burned down in 1994, I liked the way things were going enough to persevere. And just maybe, I had no choice. So I carried myself, some new cooks, some dishwashers, waiters, and musicians to our present House of Seafood on Conti Street, a three-story 1811 Creole structure.

Some days, I think I'm totally different from

my father, and other days I feel like I'm just the same. Here I am on Conti, buying or leasing anything that excites me, always looking to grow, to stay one step ahead. Through it all, wonder of wonders, my strongest ally, most reliable adviser, and, once in a while, best friend, has turned out to be my dad. Even if it was the disaster anybody with a brain would expect the one time he tried to work for me, I love having him work with me, near me, with more free advice than I can shake a crab trap at. More and more, his advice comes packaged with its own stories, most of which involve guys along the bayou who've been dead for as long as I've been alive.

Sometimes what I try works great, and other times, it's a total mess. Either way, I think, it's like driving our truck along those winding shell roads in the dark, with deep green bayous on either side. After a while, as my father has taught me, all you can do is follow the road.

Andrew Jaeger with generations of family cooks

STIRRING THE GUMBO POT

SOMETIMES, when people eat what we cook in New
Orleans, they want to know where this great stuff comes from. We
really don't mind trying to answer that question, because we sometimes ask ourselves the same thing. And the answer isn't simple.

New Orleans food is like one of those big, cast-iron gumbo pots.
Everything goes into the pot, cooks together for a long time, and eventually starts to like each other, if you know what I mean. New Orleans
is that gumbo pot, and the ingredients? The main ingredients are all of
the ethnic groups that have taken turns going into the pot. That's my
way of saying that New Orleans food is from everywhere and everybody. If you stay in this town for more than a few minutes, if you taste
something and then think and talk about what you're tasting, you're
probably already tossing something into our pot. We'll take what you
contribute and try to remember to say "thanks." After all, we've been
borrowing like this—like old-time neighbors
over the back fence—for close to 300 years.

Europeans wrote the history of New
Orleans, and in so doing, they gave the folks
who were here before them short shrift.

Two brothers, rich French Canadians
known as Iberville and Bienville, were given
the job of setting up a colony for France in
Louisiana. It was a much bigger place back
then, as Thomas Jefferson learned when he
bought it and sent Lewis and Clark out to
determine what he'd bought. Iberville and
Bienville just had to set up places to live
along the Gulf Coast. Biloxi launched the

Charles and Andrew Jaeger, Father's Day, 1997

French presence in 1699, followed by Mobile in 1704, and finally
New Orleans, on the Mississippi River, in 1719.

Bienville, it turns out, had quite a set of eyes on him, for he saw beyond the swamp, heat, bugs, and disease that New Orleans could be a great international port someday. It did indeed become such a port.

It wasn't long before some of my German ancestors showed up, though you wouldn't know it today. About 125 of them arrived in 1725 and settled across the river about 20 miles above Bienville's settlement. It was these German farmers who grew vegetables so well that the French lived through several famines that otherwise would have done them in. Within a few years, the Germans had taken French names and adopted the French language, so we know little about those early German settlers.

The French were "it" around New Orleans for quite a while, with chefs imported from the royal court in Paris. But even the best chef couldn't do much with the ingredients he found here. The smart ones learned from the local Indians, discovering grits, filé to thicken gumbo, and cornbread, and learning how to handle the seafood and game this new colony afforded them. It was a tough life, but with enough effort (and maybe enough imported Bordeaux), they could at least pretend.

However, one thing the French couldn't pretend was that Louisiana would be French forever. In 1762, Louisiana became Spanish, although it was seven more years before the Spanish showed their faces; but when they did they had quite an impact on our cooking. It was the Spanish who gave us the word "criollo" (for a child of European parents born in the colony), which eventually became the moniker for the French Creole. And it was the Spanish who taught us how to fry in lard, how to use onions and tomatoes, and how to transform our cooking with the spices they'd tasted among the Mayans, Aztecs, and Incas.

A lot of important things happened while the Spanish were in charge, and not just lessons in politics so corrupt they were (and are) the envy of the civilized world. No, first the Cajuns showed up after being uprooted from Nova Scotia.

The Cajuns (shortened from "Acadians") were mostly descendants of 400 families brought to Canada from France but expelled in the mid-1700s by the British. As ship after ship headed south, some

Cajuns got off along the East Coast, but most stayed on board until they reached New Orleans, heard their native tongue, and decided the bayou country here was the place to be.

These Cajuns, I imagine, probably went around asking somebody to pinch them to make sure they were awake. After all, they'd come from a cold and rocky place and had found a land filled with soil that grew almost anything, water from which almost anything could be dragged or persuaded, skies that were filled with birds. Cajuns then were a lot like Cajuns now; they saw just about everything in God's creation as something to eat.

Refugees from Santo Domingo (today's Haiti) were planters who loved to eat and drink, and they spoke French. The Haitians brought along not only their tropical flair but also their tropical cuisine. Finally, since Haitian rebels made a point of killing people of mixed race, as many of these people as could pull it off escaped to New Orleans. It was these folks who encouraged the idea in New Orleans that anybody can marry anybody, and it was also the Haitians who brought voodoo to the region.

Speaking of anybody marrying anybody, that's basically the way it got to be here after a while. Louisiana reverted from Spain to France under Napoleon just long enough for Napoleon to sell it to Jefferson and those rowdy Americans. Think about it: you had all kinds of immigrants coming up the river looking to be part of the promise that was America, while at the same time you had all these Americans (and not the best class of them!) coming down the river looking for a license to steal. Everybody kind of met right here, in what is known as the French Quarter. They yelled and screamed, pulled knives and pistols, went for a drink, fell down in the mud, and ended up marrying each other's sisters. If you wonder why New Orleans's food tastes as great as it does, you really have a long list of people to thank.

Records show that by 1910, my ancestors, the Germans, were the largest immigrant culture in the city. The Germans hung onto their heritage, yet they followed in the footsteps of those who came before, farming the rich river soil and selling their produce from the backs of carts. Some of these guys pulled a few dollars together and opened restaurants (then, as now, New Orleans loved restaurants), serving the sausages they made in memory of home, dishing up bowls of nose-clearing sauerkraut, trotting out huge pitchers of beer. If every day in New Orleans is a little bit of Mardi Gras, every day is a little bit of Oktoberfest, too.

All of this food and drink came together for Germans in the grocery business. Many opened small corner hangouts in neighborhoods teeming with Sicilians, Irish, Croatians, and Africans. Sure, some of these people didn't or couldn't talk to each other, but necessity forced them to "make groceries," as the French would say, side by side.

As for the Sicilians, now there's a story. These people were used to being persecuted—not only by everybody in the history of Europe but by other Italians, too. Sicilians returned the favor by refusing to be "Italian" at all, preferring to see themselves as ancient Greeks living past their prime (which in a way, they really are). The Sicilians came to New Orleans in the mid-nineteenth century to escape just about everything worth escaping: wars, famines, epidemics. They brought with them ideas about red sauce, some terrific seafood recipes, and the concept of olive salad. It was a Sicilian in New Orleans who decided that when you spread that olive salad on cold cuts and cheeses atop a crusty round loaf of bread, you had something wonderful even Sicily hadn't seen before, and thus, the muffaletta was born.

If you love seafood as I do, and if you work with seafood as my family does, you have to appreciate the Croatians. Remember them?

P & J Oyster House

When I was growing up, we called them Yugoslavs. But they were Croatians before, and now, after plenty of trouble, they're Croatians again.

Anyway, these tough workers came to low-lying southern Louisiana from the mountainous Dalmatian Coast. But for all the changes this move made, what they sought was something they knew a whole lot about. Shellfish. Especially oysters. To this day, the oyster business is dominated by small-time, independent, proud fishermen from that very old, very beautiful, very troubled part of the world.

The Irish showed up in a couple of waves, digging canals at the beginning and eventually entering politics. At my restaurant, I don't cook much that you'd consider Irish, but even the Irish in New Orleans don't cook much that's Irish.

Over the years, people of every race and culture have made New Orleans their home. And they are tied together by an unlikely and unrecognized source—the people in the kitchen. It was the people in the kitchen who made the most sense of all these wild influences, who figured out just where to borrow this and where to plug in that. Most of these people were untrained, and often illiterate, geniuses. Throughout the years in this city, all of these different people in different kitchens thought they were just making gumbo. The truth is, all those people really *were* the gumbo.

Croatian oyster fisherman
Captain John Jurisich

Captain John and Andrew Jaeger, 1999

NEW ORLEANS SEAFOOD GLOSSARY

TROUT, pompano, and redfish have long been the headliners in Louisiana fish, joined by their shelled compatriots, shrimp, oysters, crab, and crawfish. But these days you almost have to buy a program at the restaurant door to identify the kinds of fish your waiter can offer.

The past decade has seen a huge jump in U.S. seafood consumption. Red meat consumption has decreased, chicken consumption has strayed, and the air delivery of fresh fish from all over the world and the farming of seafood close to home have received a shot in the arm. These influences, combined, have increased the volume and variety of seafood that restaurants can offer year-round.

In Louisiana, fears for the survival of redfish and overfishing of speckled trout have resulted in a concerted effort to promote the glories of Louisiana tuna, swordfish, shark, black drum, and a host of other varieties that have been swimming about relatively unmolested since the beginning of time. This is great news for the mildly adventurous diner and for the balance of local ecology—even if it's bad news for these recently discovered seafood species.

If you've ever wanted to know more about what you're devouring than your waiter was able to tell you, here's the guide for you.

ALLIGATOR GAR: Garfish remains a steady seller throughout central and northern Louisiana. Garfish meat, especially that from the larger fish, is strewn with tough membranes, so it tends to be flaked for use in patties and boulettes (hand-formed balls that are deep-fried). Smoked gar is sometimes marketed, though Norwegian salmon, it's not!

BLUE CRAB: We hear a lot about Chesapeake Bay, but Louisiana is the primary shipper of live male blue crabs to the Atlantic Coast markets, with lesser amounts of mature female crabs shipped to Asian markets in Hawaii.

BLUEFISH: These fish do not tend to go over well in southern Louisiana, though they are related to the pompano and are generally popular along the Atlantic seaboard. Vast stocks swim just off the coast of Louisiana. Its dark, rather strongly flavored flesh makes it better suited for broiling than for frying.

BROWN SHRIMP: These provide the bulk of Louisiana's shrimp harvest. Sold as brown shrimp, Brazilian shrimp, or just plain "shrimp," they lack the subtle qualities associated with white shrimp, and they're generally smaller, but they are wonderful.

CHANNEL CATFISH: The new generation of farm-raised catfish have a milder taste than the wild, but both types of meat are sweet-fleshed and perfect for frying. As any sport fisher will assure you, Louisiana has more types of catfish than just about anybody would want, including blue, hardhead, yellow, and gafftopsail.

COBIA: Also known as ling or lemonfish, cobia is usually caught as a fishing by-product by snapper fishermen and deepwater shrimp trawlers. Cobia is delicious, but it is not fished or landed in great quantity.

CRAWFISH: These come in two colors and are one major obsession! The reds tend to hail from southern Louisiana, particularly from the Atchafalaya Bay, while the white are somewhat more plentiful in northern Louisiana. The meat of red or white crawfish is available in one-pound bags, fresh or frozen, either with the fat on for enhanced flavor or with the fat washed off for longer storage. Most chefs will vote "fat on" every time.

EASTERN OYSTER: Louisiana oysters vary in salt content but almost never in flavor. They are good to eat year-round, though they are at their peak of fatness between November and April.

FLORIDA POMPANO: Pompano commands the highest price of any finfish caught in Louisiana. In New Orleans, we think Florida should have to call the pompano they serve "Louisiana pompano"—but really, what's in a name? At least we can say without reservation that we are the only people who cook them in paper bags!

GROUPER: Yellowfin grouper is the most common type landed in Louisiana, followed by the huge Warsaw and the snowy. Grouper, a bottomfish, is white, lean, and flaky, perfect for just about any style of cooking. The gourmet grouper is known as "the scamp" and is caught only in small quantities.

JACK: The fish known as amberjack and crevalle jack are caught by fishers trying to get something else, yet there is a small market for them. They yield strips of dark, strong-tasting meat most suitable for broiling.

MAHIMAHI: Known on our docks as dolphin or dolphinfish (to prevent confusion of this fish with the mammal we know as Flipper), mahimahi has a flaky, almost-white flesh that makes it a great fish for broiling, as more and more diners are coming to recognize.

PINK SHRIMP: Sometimes called "hoppers," these are actually a bycatch of the brown shrimp harvest. Pink shrimp taste more like brown shrimp than white, despite their unique coloration.

RED DRUM: This is the official name of Louisiana's redfish. Happily, chefs and diners are awakening to the fact that the black drum is pretty similar to the red drum—and much more readily available.

RED SNAPPER: Here's a real workhorse in restaurants. It is great cooked in virtually any manner with virtually any sauce. Fillets are usually sold skin-on to deter people from trying to sell inferior fish as red snapper. Louisiana waters also produce blackfin snappers, lane snappers, vermilion snappers, queen snappers, and gray snappers, all of which are good to eat.

SHARK: At least nine varieties of shark are fished in Louisiana waters. They are found along the entire coast, but are fished mostly out of Grand Isle and Venice. The mako, quite close to swordfish in taste and texture, is the preferred type, followed at a distance by bull, Atlantic sharpnose, and silky. Shark meat is very white, lean, and versatile. It is also boneless.

SHEEPSHEAD: This is a very common Louisiana fish with white, lean flesh that reminds many of crabmeat. Sheepshead can be cooked successfully in a wide variety of ways.

SOFTSHELL CRABS: The state's softshell crabs tend to draw a higher price than softshells from any other state. Backfin, or jumbo lump meat, is the most expensive among four types of picked meat; it comes in the largest lumps and includes the fewest shell fragments.

SOUTHERN FLOUNDER: Flounder has the leanest, driest flesh of any fish caught in Louisiana. The absence of moisture makes it perfect for freezing; ice crystals, which cut the flesh and turn it to mush, don't tend to form, so it can easily be enjoyed anytime. Flounder is often served stuffed, but it is great simply broiled with a light sprinkling of pepper.

SPECKLED TROUT: Known officially as the spotted sea trout or even weakfish, the "speck" is historically the number one commercial fish in Louisiana's saltwater marshes. Terrific to catch and terrific to eat, this fish has been the subject of survival concerns in recent years. The supply seems to be doing better, thanks to federal limits on the catch.

SQUID: Both long-finned and short-finned varieties remain a bycatch of the shrimp industry. They tend to turn up in nets between May and December, going with great rapidity either to Italian cooks or to those of Vietnamese and Thai descent living in New Orleans.

STONE CRAB: Stone crabs turn up in the crab traps along with the blue crabs. They are marketed in limited amounts and don't tend to be sold beyond the local market.

SWORDFISH: Like tuna, swordfish came into its own with the adoption of grilling as a favorite cooking technique of many chefs. Its large, firm steaks work wonderfully this way.

WAHOO: The name of this fish, a type of mackerel, fits right in with New Orleans's fabled party atmosphere—too bad its meat tends not to. Wahoo is enjoyed, however, by fans of mackerel. The flesh of wahoo tends to be oily, but unlike other mackerel, is generally light.

WHITE SHRIMP: You'll see these sold sometimes as Gulf prawns, though they're technically not prawns. These are Louisiana's premium large shrimp, and they almost always draw the highest price in the markets. Their qualities include tenderness of meat, ease of peeling, and the absence of the slight iodine flavor sometimes associated with shrimp.

YELLOWFIN TUNA: Yellowfin has only been caught here since 1980, and it is now a major crop. The best yellowfin is sold for the "sashimi trade," to be eaten raw in Japanese restaurants. But all yellowfin is excellent, particularly when marinated and grilled. Less expensive but similar in quality are the bluefin and blackfin tunas that are also caught in Louisiana waters.

JUST about everybody who grew up in New Orleans has some kind of shrimping experience. I had more than most people, naturally, with my father being in the business and so many relatives owning boats. But some of my earliest memories of shrimping don't even involve a boat. We used to pull castnets full of flopping shrimp right out of Lake Pontchartrain, shrimping in the evenings from the concrete steps we called "the seawall," though we were a fair distance from the sea.

Done right, shrimping is an all-day or all-night affair. Back in my seawall days, most folks would start in the morning by catching the little clams that grow in the lake. Few people know we have clams here in Louisiana, but we do, and they're at least tasty enough to make shrimp happy. The idea is you catch a bunch of clams, chop them all up, and throw them into the lake as bait. The shrimp find their way in to feed on all these clams, and before you know it, they're flopping around on the seawall in your castnet.

I should point out that using a castnet requires a good bit of skill. Most people get the hang of it eventually since it doesn't require any major smarts, but it does require practice. The movements involved seem to belong to another, more primitive time and place, and probably they do. I can't give you a lesson here in the fine art of casting around swimming shrimp, and jerking the net right and then left so it closes just perfectly around them, but I can show you sometime if you ask me.

Another way we caught shrimp was with a trawl net. We'd pull a trawl net behind a boat we called a Lafitte skiff. The skiff was named after our local pirate, Jean Lafitte, or rather, it was named after the town that was named after the pirate. The town turned out these skiffs like there was no tomorrow. (Of course, when you were cooking in a restaurant all day and trawling for shrimp all night, there really didn't seem to be a tomorrow.)

When we were young, my brother, Allen, and I would take our Lafitte skiff into the bayous and bays and marshes after a full day in our family's restaurant. We used every trick our ancestors ever thought of: eighteen-foot trawls, plus twelve-foot butterfly nets that look like graceful wings sprouting from the side of your boat, and all kinds of so-called night rigging. Sometimes, when there was still a little daylight at the falling of the tide, or when there was a bright, glassy moon shining on the water, you see'd the shrimp moving across the surface like a waving "S." They were riding the current out, and it was your job, as the old-timers put it, to push against the falling tide. It was hard work, since everything in nature was trying to pull you the other way, and sooner or later, you had to bring in the nets.

These days, machines help, but I remember when we had to do it all manually. I'll never forget this cousin of mine called Sonny. He had huge arms (a side benefit of shrimping, in those days before Nautilus machines!), and he was incredibly strong. We would watch Sonny pull in those shrimp nets from the water behind the boat, starting with the heavy waterlogged boards that helped spread the nets out wide and working his way back to the heavy knot that (you hoped) held all those shrimp.

When shrimping, you were always at the beck and call of the tides, whether you kept up by reading (New Orleans newspapers and TV stations still give the tidal reports every day) or by listening to the old people, who always knew, or could tell, or could guess. These folks were never wrong about much that involved water or rain or wind, anything that made the difference between thousands of dollars and burning a tankful of fuel for six shrimp, a gafftopsail catfish, and a couple of oyster shells. They always knew what was happening out there in the marsh.

Although I remember some very disappointing trips, when I think of the nights we started trawling at ten o'clock, and didn't pull in the nets until two or three in the morning, I mostly remember excitement. There was always some kind of surprise in the net—and sometimes a quite painful one. One time, when I wasn't as careful as I should have been, I reached into this mound of shrimp only to have the stiff, sharp spike atop a catfish pierce my hand. Catfish were the constant threat to your bounty, much more than the occasional stingray. You learned to be careful at a young age.

Still, if you learned one cut and one poke and one puncture at a time, you never lost that little quickness of breath every time you pulled in that net. You didn't know what you had; you could never know. Mostly, what you had in there was money. But it didn't look or act or feel like money. It looked and acted and felt like magic.

NOT QUITE AS EASY AS BOILING WATER

If you think of boiling seafood as nothing more than putting shrimp, crabs, or crawfish in hot, bubbling water, you haven't been living in New Orleans. A whole set of traditions has grown up around the New Orleans seafood boil, and a fair chunk of solid science as well. We can't write the science down as some kind of formula, but we can do it right—and teach others to do it right—generation after generation.

At my family's restaurant on Elysian Fields, little was taken more seriously than boiled seafood. My dad never stopped tweaking his spice recipe or buying some new gadget that was supposed to boil better. I look on boiling seafood as a creative adventure every time. Still, there are things I know to be true. And I'm passing them on to you.

First, you need to make a party worth boiling seafood for. If you hate people, hate music, and hate having fun, really, why put yourself to all the trouble? You need a bunch of beer and a bunch of people, and preferably people you enjoy drinking beer with. New Orleans beers, like Dixie (and even Abita from the north shore of Lake Pontchartrain), are best. You need newspaper to cover anything off of which you might be tempted to eat. Our own *Times-Picayune* makes material for this, but your local paper would probably do. And you need music, New Orleans music. The Neville Brothers are hard to beat to accompany a seafood boil. The Radiators and Dr. John are good, too. These guys supply the kind of funky, gyrating soul that somehow makes seafood taste better than anything else on earth. Beer, music, newspaper, and good people, and you're most of the way home.

In New Orleans, the key to the flavor of boiled seafood is not just using the freshest main ingredients, but applying the best spices to the water. I know that places in the Northeast and Northwest think they do like we do with boiled seafood, but you'll have to taste and be the judge. I don't know of any place that uses the vibrancy of spices we include in the mix we call "crab boil." (We call it crab boil even if there's not a crab in sight. It keeps us from fretting over incidentals, and the shrimp or crawfish we're boiling don't act like they're insulted.) Now, you can buy excellent crab boil mixed commercially here in New Orleans. If you can find anything by Yogi or Zatarain's, you're onto the real thing.

Once you've got your spices right (we've included a good New Orleans recipe, in case your stores don't carry the right stuff), you need to worry about the cooking itself. There aren't too many worse things you can do to seafood than to overboil it. And since shrimp are more delicate than crabs and crawfish, you need to consider the differences once you set to boiling. After the seafood has boiled the few minutes required, let it steep in the hot (but no longer boiling) water, busy as can be, soaking up spice. When boiling shrimp, we always dump a cup or two of ice cubes into the boil once the steeping has begun. This brings the temperature down just right so the shrimp don't over-cook. With hard-shelled crabs and crawfish, this quick-cooling isn't necessary.

Seafood is the main event at a seafood boil, but you can add peeled new potatoes and corn on the cob to the water if you like. You may not know how much "hot" potatoes and corn can happily, and deliciously, suck up.

When everything is cooked and drained and perfect, and when the cook has been compensated with at least one beer, it's time to dump (daintily spooning anything is NOT allowed in New Orleans) the bright seafood and its accompaniments onto sections of the newspaper. If you choose your seating according to preferred topic, you might even be able to catch up on the news!

NOTE: The way I like to eat is to taste a variety of different textures and flavors. We have no rules in New Orleans on how to eat and in what combinations, so feel free to use any of these shrimp dishes as entrées or sides. Why not just make eight or ten of them, crank up the music, and have your own Louisiana shrimp festival? P.S. Be sure to invite me!

Shrimp Remoulade

Serves 4 as an appetizer

Remoulade Sauce

2 anchovy fillets

½ tablespoon freshly
squeezed lemon juice

½ cup mayonnaise

½ cup Creole mustard

1 teaspoon white wine

1 dash of Tabasco sauce

½ cup paprika

3 to 4 heads iceberg let-
tuce, shredded

24 medium (36 to 40
count) shrimp, boiled
and peeled (page 29)

4 lemon wedges

Remoulade is a classic in New Orleans as it is in France. However, as you might have already guessed, our remoulade isn't anything like theirs. Theirs comes either in a white or green herbal mix or in a thick sauce resembling mayonnaise. New Orleans opts to emphasize our pungent, sinus-clearing Creole mustard. We actually have two kinds of remoulade of our own, one, a golden brown, and the other tending toward red. This recipe comes out more red than brown, with the anchovy fillets adding a marvelous depth of flavor. The sauce works well with boiled shrimp, but it is also good as a dip for any boiled seafood or for a memorable salad dressing.

T0 prepare the sauce, place the anchovy fillets in a bowl and add the lemon juice. Mash the fillets with the juice until a paste is formed. Add the remaining ingredients and mix well. Place the sauce in the refrigerator to chill for 3 hours before serving.

To serve, make a bed of lettuce on each of 4 appetizer plates. Place about 6 boiled shrimp on the lettuce and top with the remoulade sauce. Serve with a lemon wedge on each plate.

Skillet Shrimp

Serves 4

32 jumbo (16 to 20 count)
shrimp, peeled and
deveined

2 teaspoons blackening
seasoning (page 145)

3 tablespoons unsalted
butter, melted

Cooking shrimp doesn't have to be difficult or time-consuming. In fact, when you're dealing with something that tastes so good, some-times the less you do to it, the better. We think you'll enjoy this easy nibble, sided perhaps with garlic pasta or a simple rice dish. For a real treat, you might top these shrimp with creamy crab sauce (page 147).

HEAT a cast-iron skillet to high. Sprinkle the peeled shrimp with the seasoning and toss in a bowl to coat evenly. Dip the shrimp in the melted butter and place in the hot skillet. Cook for 2 to 3 min-utes, turning to cook all sides evenly. Serve the shrimp topped with creamy crab sauce.

Seafood Boil

Serves 6 to 10

Major traditions and techniques have developed around the high art of boiling seafood in New Orleans, with shrimp leading the way, followed by crabs and, of course, crawfish. You can add more vegetables too (see note).

BRING water to a boil in a stockpot. Mix the spices and add them, plus the onions, garlic, and celery to the water, and return to a rolling boil. Lower the heat to a light boil and cook, uncovered, for 30 minutes. Add the shrimp and return to a rolling boil. Boil for 3 minutes, or until the shrimp rise to the surface. Turn off the heat and add the salt. Add 3 or 4 trays of ice to stop the boiling process. Let the shrimp stand in the broth as it cools for 20 minutes. Drain the shrimp and serve on large platters or newspaper.

NOTES: You can use this same recipe for crab and crawfish, with a few changes. When cooking crab and crawfish, the salt should be added at the beginning of the process, with the spices and vegetables. Bring the crab or crawfish to a boil for 5 minutes and let stand in hot broth for 30 minutes. Do not add ice to the mixture.

To add corn on the cob, new potatoes, whole artichokes, or smoked sausage to the boil, remove the seafood from the pot, reserving the water, spices, and cooked vegetables. Add the new ingredients and boil them as you would normally cook corn or potatoes. The sausage will plump up when ready and you will be able to easily pull off a leaf of the artichoke. It is highly recommended to boil all seafood and vegetables separately for best results.

When making any recipe that calls for boiled peeled shrimp, you will get the best flavor from fresh head-on shrimp that have been boiled, chilled, and peeled using the above method. But when in a hurry, you can use frozen peeled shrimp and get good results.

For those of you who must know, you'll get 50 to 60 small shrimp in a pound, 36 to 40 medium, 21 to 25 large, and 16 to 20 jumbo.

1½ gallons water

Spice Mixture

¼ cup whole allspice

1 tablespoon black peppercorns

1 tablespoon crushed red pepper flakes

10 bay leaves

1 teaspoon whole cloves

1 tablespoon dill seed

2 tablespoons mustard seed

1 tablespoon coriander seed

¾ cup cayenne pepper

3 onions, halved

3 bulbs garlic, halved crosswise

4 ribs celery, quartered

5 pounds shrimp, any size (preferably with head on)

1 cup salt

Quick Boiled Shrimp

If you don't have time to boil fresh shrimp, use frozen shrimp. Bring 2 cups water to a boil with 2 tablespoons blackening seasoning, 1 whole lemon cut in half, 5 peppercorns, and 1 tablespoon salt. Add the shrimp, cook for 2 minutes, then drain and cool.

Gulf Shrimp Gazpacho

1 cup small (50 to 60 count) cooked shrimp, peeled

1 green bell pepper, seeded and diced

1 red bell pepper, seeded and diced

1 small yellow onion, finely chopped

1 small rib celery, finely chopped

2 teaspoons minced garlic

4½ cups V-8 juice

1 (10-ounce) can beef broth

1 tablespoon Worcestershire sauce

1 teaspoon hot pepper sauce

1 teaspoon ground cumin

Salt and freshly ground black pepper

2 cucumbers, peeled, seeded, and diced

Serves 8

If you're in the mood for soup but are afraid it will get you hot under the collar, never fear. I take a hint from the Spanish classic gazpacho, except that I give the chilled concoction character by adding some fresh Gulf shrimp.

COMBINE the shrimp and all of the vegetables except the cucumbers in a large saucepan. Stir in the V-8 juice, beef broth, and Worcestershire sauce, and add the hot pepper sauce and cumin. Season to taste with salt and pepper. Bring just to a simmer over medium heat, and then immediately remove from the heat and let cool. Refrigerate in a tightly sealed plastic container for at least 12 hours. Remove from the refrigerator, add the diced cucumbers, and serve cold.

Sicilian Eggplant with Shrimp

Serves 6 as an appetizer; serves 4 as an entrée

This dish goes straight to the heart of New Orleans's Sicilian heritage and shows Sicily's profound debt to the Greeks across the water. This is one of the best eggplant dishes I've ever tasted. It has evolved into a New Orleans dish, first and foremost, because New Orleans is quick to absorb anything it really loves, and second, because the shrimp adds a fresh taste of the Gulf. The shrimp and eggplant sauté is terrific served over rice or cooked pasta (linguine works great) or used as a topping to add color and excitement to a simple fish or grilled chicken breast.

IN a large sauté pan, heat the oil over medium-high heat and add the eggplant. Cook for 3 to 4 minutes, stirring constantly. Add the tomatoes and garlic and sauté for 3 to 4 minutes more, until the eggplants soften. Add the remaining ingredients and lower the heat to medium. Cook until the eggplants are completely soft and the shrimp are pink. Serve hot.

1/3 cup extra virgin olive oil

3 eggplants, peeled and cut in 1/2-inch cubes

3 cups whole peeled tomatoes, with juice

1 tablespoon minced garlic

2 pounds peeled and cleaned medium (36 to 40 count) shrimp

2/3 cup marsala wine

2 teaspoons Italian seasoning (page 149)

1 loosely packed table-spoon chopped fresh basil

3 tablespoons capers, thoroughly rinsed and drained

1 teaspoon Tabasco sauce

1/2 teaspoon salt

How to Peel Shrimp

Peeling shrimp is probably the easiest thing in the bag of tricks required to eat New Orleans seafood, perhaps because so many people have peeled at least one shrimp sometime in their lives. So, let's start here.

Boiled or raw, shrimp require only the most basic flirtation to get them out of their clothes. We respect that attitude here in New Orleans. The standard method for peeling shrimp involves holding the shrimp in one hand and using the other hand to twist off the head and all of the various whiskers. This leaves the body with a whole bunch of little legs holding the shell together at the bottom. Remove these legs and the shell enclosing the body like a horse's blanket is ready to come off. Once the shell is removed, the tail can easily be twisted off. But don't let too much of the tail meat get away.

As we describe in our look at a New Orleans seafood boil (pages 26–27 and 29), the primary advantage of peeling shrimp once they're boiled is that it leaves all but your fingers free to enjoy the important things in life: family, music, and beer. Practice can really improve your speed so that you will have a definite Darwinian advantage in any newspaper-lined New Orleans feeding frenzy.

Peeling raw shrimp will strike most first-timers as both harder and messier than peeling boiled shrimp, but it's not. Use the same method as for peeling boiled shrimp. The only difference is the shrimp meat will be greenish brown rather than a lovely reddish orange, and the various juices are less appetizing. But hey, you're not peeling raw shrimp for good looks, you're peeling them for good food.

Finally, there are traditions surrounding what to discard and when to discard it. I know cookbooks all over America devein all shrimp as a matter of course. In New Orleans we see nothing wrong with the dark little line that runs along the back of a shrimp and generally don't bother deveining much of anything. The only real exceptions to this rule are jumbo shrimp, which cook best butterflied anyway.

The other discardable part of a shrimp is the head, but generations of cooks have warned us not to be hasty. The head of a shrimp (like the head of a crawfish) carries an immense amount of flavor, probably more than any other part of the creature. If you're boiling shrimp and can get your hands on whole ones, don't get rid of the heads until after the boil—the boiling water will become a spicy, shrimpy treasure! And if you're making anything resembling our New Orleans Barbecued Shrimp (page 40), do sauté these babies with the heads on. Once again, the fat will infuse the buttery sauce with goodness you can never get from a shrimp that has lost its head.

Coconut Shrimp with Citrus Sauce

Serves 4 as an appetizer

Citrus Sauce

1 tablespoon puréed
  pickled ginger

1 tablespoon lime zest
  (colored part only,
  leaving bitter white)

1 tablespoon lemon zest
  (colored part only,
  leaving bitter white)

2 tablespoons orange
  zest (colored part only,
  leaving bitter white)

Juice of 1 orange

Juice of 1 lemon

$^{1}/_{2}$ cup rice wine vinegar

12 jumbo (16 to 20 count)
  shrimp, peeled,
  deveined, and
  butterflied

2 eggs

1$^{1}/_{2}$ cups seasoned flour
  (page 145)

1 cup dark beer

$^{1}/_{2}$ cup shredded coconut

1 cup honey

1 tablespoon Asian chile
  paste or 1 tablespoon
  crushed red pepper
  blended with oil

1 cup firmly packed dark
  brown sugar

Vegetable oil for deep-
  frying

There's something about coconut in New Orleans. It keeps turning up in dishes, as though to remind us how many links we have to the islands to our south. Here's a dish that's become very popular in the last few years. Some people make it like it's an Asian dish, while others make it like it's a Caribbean dish. I, naturally, make it like both.

TO prepare the citrus sauce marinade, combine all of the ingredients for the citrus sauce in a large bowl. Add the shrimp, cover, and marinate for 1 hour in the refrigerator.

To prepare the batter, beat the eggs into the seasoned flour in a separate large bowl and add the beer and coconut.

Remove the shrimp from the refrigerator. Pour the marinade from the shrimp into a skillet and add the honey, chile paste, and brown sugar. Reduce over medium-high heat by about half, 4 to 5 minutes. Dip the shrimp into the batter, holding each by the tail, and deep-fry in cooking oil preheated to 350 degrees in a deep-fryer until golden brown. Remove the shrimp from the hot oil with a slotted spoon and set on paper towels to drain. To each of 4 appetizer plates, transfer 3 of the fried shrimp and spoon some of the warm citrus sauce over the shrimp. Serve immediately.

Sautéed Sesame Shrimp

Serves 4 as an appetizer; serves 2 as an entrée

The sesame oil gives this dish a little kick in the pants from the Orient, as does the sherry. But I wasn't really trying to come up with something Asian—just something good. Considering the number of requests we get for this dish, especially as an appetizer, we must be doing something right.

MIX together the ingredients for the marinade in a large bowl and add the shrimp. Toss to coat the shrimp thoroughly (about 100 times). Cover and refrigerate for 1 hour.

In a large skillet over medium heat, add the marinated shrimp and cook, stirring constantly, until pink, about 3 minutes. Do not let the garlic burn. Pour in the sherry and scrape up browned bits from the pan and continue to cook until the sherry is almost evaporated.

To toast the sesame seeds, place in a hot skillet over medium heat, tossing until they start to brown, about 1 minute.

To serve, divide the lettuce evenly among the plates. Place the shrimp on the bed of lettuce and top with the sesame seeds and green onions.

Marinade

2 tablespoons sesame oil

2 tablespoons chopped garlic

1/2 teaspoon blackening seasoning (page 145)

1/2 teaspoon salt

1/4 teaspoon Tabasco sauce

2 cups peeled jumbo (16 to 20 count) shrimp, peeled, deveined, butterflied, and drained well

2/3 cup dry sherry

1 tablespoon sesame seeds, for garnish

1/2 head iceberg lettuce, shredded

1/4 cup thinly sliced green onions, for garnish

Marinated Italian Shrimp Salad

1 cup boiled medium (36 to 40 count) shrimp (page 29), peeled, or plain shrimp boiled with salt and pepper

2 teaspoons chopped garlic

½ cup olives, drained

6 tablespoons extra virgin olive oil

3 thin lemon slices, cut and quartered (about ⅓ lemon)

1 tablespoon capers, rinsed and drained

¼ teaspoon coarsely ground black pepper

¼ head iceberg lettuce, shredded

Serves 4

This is my mother's recipe, drawn from decade after decade of New Orleans' seafood culture. Like several others of our shrimp recipes, it also works great with crab (cracked open in the shell to absorb all of the flavor) and with crawfish with only the heads removed. You might even borrow a trick from my mother, tossing the leaves of freshly boiled artichokes into the marinade right along with the seafood.

TOSS all of the ingredients except the lettuce together for 3 to 4 minutes. Cover and refrigerate for 1 hour. Serve cold over shredded lettuce.

Shrimp Tasso Pasta

Serves 8 as an appetizer; serves 4 as an entrée

I don't believe the Cajuns have been cooking this dish forever, but you'd sure think they have been from the way they gobble it up now. The key is that the intensely smoky and heavily seasoned flavor of the tasso is smoothed out by reduced heavy cream. In this case, I think you'll agree, reduction equals seduction. Tasso is a Cajun smoked, spiced, and cured pork. A spicy, cured sausage can be substituted.

I N a medium saucepan over medium heat, melt the butter and add the shrimp, tasso, and blackening seasoning. Cook, stirring constantly, until the shrimp are pink, 1 to 2 minutes. Add the garlic and cream and reduce by half over medium-high heat, stirring constantly, about 5 minutes. Add the pasta and green onions and toss to heat the pasta. Season to taste with salt and black pepper and sprinkle with the cheese. Toss again and serve immediately.

2 tablespoons unsalted butter

1 cup peeled medium (36 to 40 count) shrimp

2 heaping tablespoons tasso

2 tablespoons blackening seasoning (page 145)

1 teaspoon chopped garlic

2 cups heavy whipping cream

16 ounces cooked linguine

1/4 cup finely chopped green onions

Salt and coarsely ground black pepper

1 cup grated pecorino-romano cheese

Stuffed Shrimp

Serves 12 as an appetizer; serves 4 as an entrée

12 jumbo (16 to 20 count) shrimp, peeled, deveined, and butter-flied (tails on)

1⅓ cups crab stuffing (page 70)

About 1 cup Italian-style bread crumbs

1 cup brandy cream sauce (page 147)

This one may take a little practice, since the procedure involves partly stuffing into the shrimp and partly molding stuffing around the shrimp. But it will be worth it. Besides, once you learn how to make one good New Orleans stuffing, you can stuff anything in sight, from these shrimp to crab to lobster, and even fish, like our delicate flounder.

PREHEAT the oven to 400 degrees.

Stuff each shrimp with some of the crab stuffing, using your hands to shape the mixture in a tapered mound, like a football. Sprinkle the bread crumbs over the shrimp, pressing it in with your hands, and place the shrimp, stuffed side down, on a baking sheet coated with olive oil. Bake in the oven at 350 degrees for 20 minutes, or until the shrimp are cooked. Remove the shrimp from the oven, place on a plate, and top with about 1 tablespoon of the brandy cream sauce.

Shrimp Kebabs

Serves 4

Marinade

1 cup extra virgin olive oil

1 tablespoon chopped garlic

1 teaspoon Italian seasoning (page 149)

1 teaspoon red pepper flakes

3 fresh basil leaves

24 jumbo (16 to 20 count) shrimp, peeled

2 large red onions, quartered

2 green bell peppers, cut in 2-inch squares

8 cherry tomatoes

This dish can be made indoors or out with equally impressive results. If you are outside, it does make one heck of a picnic item. Remember—if you're using wooden skewers, be sure to soak them in water for 10 to 15 minutes before using to keep them from catching fire on the barbecue.

IN a large glass bowl, mix together all of the ingredients for the marinade. Place the shrimp, onions, green peppers, and cherry tomatoes on skewers, ending with an onion at the top of the skewer. Place the kebabs in the pan with the marinade, cover with plastic wrap, and refrigerate for 3 hours. Grill over medium-high heat for about 3 minutes, or broil for 5 minutes at 400 degrees. Place on dinner plates and remove the skewers.

Shrimp Scampi

Serves 4

I was never trained in classic Italian cooking, but growing up around my mother's kitchen, I sure learned to love the taste. This recipe takes what I've seen of Italian technique and applies it to how we like to eat here in New Orleans.

SAUTÉ the garlic in the olive oil in a large pan over medium-high heat about 1 minute. Add the shrimp and the remaining ingredients except the garlic butter. Reduce by half, about 4 minutes, and then stir in the garlic butter until the mixture is smooth and creamy. Serve immediately.

NOTE: I like to serve this and barbecued shrimp with plenty of hot, crusty French bread. Try a little of the garlic butter on your bread.

1 teaspoon chopped garlic

2 tablespoons extra virgin olive oil

12 jumbo (16 to 20 count) shrimp, peeled and butterflied

1/4 teaspoon Italian seasoning (page 149)

1/4 teaspoon coarsely ground black pepper

2 tablespoons finely chopped green onions

1 cup chopped button mushrooms

2/3 cup dry white wine

2 teaspoons freshly squeezed lemon juice

1/4 teaspoon red pepper flakes

1/4 teaspoon salt

1/4 cup garlic butter (page 146) or regular butter, melted

Barbecued Shrimp

Serves 4

2 tablespoons melted butter

12 jumbo (16 to 20 count) shrimp, shells on

1 teaspoon coarsely ground black pepper

1/2 teaspoon Worcestershire sauce

2 tablespoons white wine

1 bay leaf

1/4 teaspoon Tabasco sauce

1/4 cup garlic butter (page 146) or regular butter, melted

Quite a few restaurants in New Orleans serve some version of barbecued shrimp, which is built around shrimp but has nothing to do with anybody's idea of barbecue. We seem to take words, spellings, and definitions here pretty lightly, but no one can ever say we take flavor lightly. By the way, you can do what you like, but we always make this dish with the heads on the shrimp. The taste advantage is extraordinary.

HEAT the butter in a large saucepan over medium-high heat. Add the shrimp and sauté just until pink, 2 to 3 minutes. Add all of the remaining ingredients except the garlic butter and sauté until the wine is reduced by about half, 6 to 7 minutes. Stir in the garlic butter until the mixture is smooth and creamy, remove the bay leaf, and serve immediately.

NOTE: The secret to this dish is plenty of black pepper and butter. If you can take it, don't be afraid to add more. And for a different dimension, throw the wine out and add some Dixie beer. Now that's a party.

Fried Shrimp

Serves 8 as an appetizer; serves 4 as an entrée

Frying may be a lost art in some cities, but not in New Orleans. Just follow these instructions carefully, right down to the temperature of the oil, and you'll end up with perfect fried shrimp every time. There are a variety of large and small deep-fryers on the market these days; consider buying one if you're going to fry shrimp and other seafood on a regular basis.

TO prepare the whitewash, use a whisk to beat together the egg, milk, and flour in a medium bowl until incorporated and smooth.

In a separate bowl, mix together all of the ingredients for the coating. Dip each shrimp in the whitewash, and then add the shrimp to the bowl with the coating mix and toss. Fry in oil preheated to 350 degrees in a deep-fryer until the shrimp float to the top, or until golden brown, about 2 minutes. Drain on paper towels and serve hot.

NOTE: To make a great fried shrimp sandwich, slice lengthwise an 8-inch piece of French bread and butter both sides with garlic butter (page 146). Mound 1 side with fried shrimp, the other with sliced tomatoes, shredded lettuce, and sliced dill pickle. Place on a baking sheet in a 400-degree oven for 3 to 4 minutes, or until the bread starts to brown. Remove from the oven, cut in half, and place on a plate with sides of cocktail sauce (page 146), Crystal hot sauce, and a cold root beer.

Whitewash

1 egg

2 cups milk

1/4 cup seasoned flour (page 145)

Coating

1 cup cornmeal

1/2 cup all-purpose flour

1/4 teaspoon ground allspice

1/2 teaspoon celery salt

1/2 teaspoon freshly ground black pepper

1/2 teaspoon freshly ground red pepper

1 teaspoon salt

1/2 teaspoon garlic powder

1 pound medium (36 to 40 count) shrimp, peeled and deveined

Vegetable oil for deep-frying

Blackened Shrimp with Creamy Fettucine

Serves 4

Everybody knows blackened redfish—especially the redfish, which needed federal protection to survive when this dish became a national mania in the 1980s. Blackened redfish is no longer a mania, but the technique is still fabulous for delivering a blast of Louisiana flavors. The spiciness of these shrimp is balanced nicely by the creaminess of the pasta.

PUT the melted butter in a medium bowl. Dip each shrimp in the butter and sprinkle the shrimp generously with some of the blackening seasoning. Heat a large sauté pan until it is almost smoking and add the shrimp. Blacken for 2 to 3 minutes, until the shrimp are flecked with the spicy char. Remove the shrimp and drain off any residual butter on paper towels.

Add the cream and ¹/₂ tablespoon of the blackening seasoning to the pan and reduce the cream by half over medium-high heat, about 4 minutes. Add the green peppers, cheese, and fettucine and toss until the pasta is thoroughly coated. Place some of the pasta on each plate and place 3 shrimp on top of the pasta. Serve immediately.

¹/₄ cup butter, melted

12 jumbo (16 to 20 count) shrimp, peeled, deveined, and butterflied

¹/₄ cup blackening seasoning (page 145)

1 cup heavy cream

4 tablespoons finely chopped green bell peppers

¹/₄ cup grated pecorino-romano cheese

1 pound cooked fettucine

Creole Shrimp Salad

Serves 6 to 8

In New Orleans, as elsewhere, great salads are born when someone needs to find new life for leftovers. In this case, let's presume you've had a terrific Seafood Boil (page 29), but ended up with some of everything left. You can just keep nibbling (and loving it!) day after day. Or you can make this flavorful salad.

PUT all of the ingredients except the lettuce in a large bowl, mix together, and marinate in the refrigerator 1 hour. Serve cold over a bed of shredded lettuce.

NOTE: Creole mustard is a spicy brown mustard made in New Orleans. You can substitute any coarse-ground brown mustard.

1 pound medium (36 to 40 count) shrimp, boiled, peeled, and deveined

1 pound new potatoes, diced and boiled

1/2 cup fresh corn kernels, cooked

1/4 cup finely chopped green onions

1/3 cup boiled egg whites, chopped

1/4 cup chopped celery

2 tablespoons chopped fresh parsley

2 tablespoons Creole mustard

1/2 cup mayonnaise

1 tablespoon freshly squeezed lemon juice

1/2 head iceberg lettuce, shredded

Stock

3 pounds fresh medium
(36 to 40 count)
shrimp, heads on

2 quarts water

1/2 cup chopped onions

1/2 cup chopped green
bell peppers

1/2 cup chopped celery

3 bay leaves

1/2 cup butter

1 cup chopped onions

1 cup chopped green bell
peppers

1 cup chopped celery

1/4 cup margarine

1/4 cup all-purpose flour

1 cup water

1/4 liquid crab boil or 1
tablespoon seafood
boil mix (page 29)

1 tablespoon Crystal hot
sauce or other
Louisiana hot sauce

2 bay leaves

1/2 teaspoon Tabasco
sauce

1/4 teaspoon freshly
ground black pepper

Whitewash (page 148)

2 tablespoons sherry

1 1/2 teaspoons salt

1 teaspoon
Worcestershire sauce

1 cup chopped green
onions

3 cups steamed white rice

Cajun Shrimp Stew

Serves 6 to 8

This dish clearly contrasts Cajun and Creole cooking, those two indigenous styles that people tend to confuse. A Creole seeking a meal like this would make Shrimp Creole, and we'll give you the recipe for that wonderful dish, too (page 45). A Cajun would jump right in and make this stew. It has a lot of ingredients; but like most of the best Cajun cooking, it's surprisingly easy and incredibly forgiving.

T 0 make the stock, peel and clean the shrimp, reserving the heads and peelings. Set the shrimp aside. Place the shrimp heads, peels, water, onions, bell peppers, celery, and bay leaves in a stockpot over high heat. Bring to a boil, stirring occasionally. Continue to cook until reduced by half, 20 to 30 minutes. Strain the liquid and reserve.

Prepare a dark roux by heating the margarine in a heavy skillet over medium heat. Whisk in the flour. Cook, stirring constantly, until dark brown, 8 to 10 minutes. The roux should be the color of coffee grounds. Remove from the heat but continue to stir. Set aside.

To make the stew, melt the butter in a large pot over medium heat. Add the onions, bell peppers, and celery and cook until the vegetables are soft. Add half of the peeled shrimp, stirring occasionally, and cook until the shrimp are pink and tender, about 2 minutes. Add the roux and 4 cups of the stock, stirring constantly, until the roux is completely dissolved. Add the water, liquid crab boil, Crystal hot sauce, bay leaves, Tabasco, black pepper, whitewash, sherry, salt, and Worcestershire, and bring the mixture to a boil, stirring constantly, until the liquid thickens. Add the remaining shrimp and the green onions. Mix well, and then lower the heat to a simmer and cook about 10 minutes.

Serve hot over steamed white rice.

Shrimp Creole

Serves 10

*This is the Creole rendition of the same basic idea as Cajun Shrimp
Stew. The most obvious difference is that this dish is bright red—
courtesy of the Spaniards and their addition of tomatoes into the
local obsession. Beyond that, there are subtle differences in seasoning.
The best news is this Creole sauce is great with any seafood or with
chunks of chicken. The latter is so flavorful, in fact, that Chicken
Creole is a real local dish, not just a convenient substitute for shrimp.*

MELT the butter over medium heat in a large pan. Add the onions
and peppers and cook, stirring constantly, until they are soft, 5 to
6 minutes. Increase heat to high; add the seasonings, Worcestershire sauce, tomatoes, and chicken stock; and bring to a boil.

Add the whitewash to the sauce. Add the sherry, hot sauce,
and shrimp to the pot and continue boiling for about 5 minutes,
just until the shrimp are cooked. Serve immediately over steamed
white rice.

- 1 cup butter
- 8 cups chopped onions
- 8 cups chopped green bell peppers
- 2 tablespoons Italian seasoning (page 149)
- 2 tablespoons ground black pepper
- 2 tablespoons blackening seasoning (page 145)
- 2 1/3 cups Worcestershire sauce
- 16 cups chopped canned tomatoes (with juice)
- 2 quarts chicken stock (page 149)
- 2 1/2 cups basic whitewash (page 148)
- 1 cup sherry
- 3 tablespoons Crystal hot sauce or other Louisiana hot sauce
- 3 pounds medium (36 to 40 count) shrimp, peeled and deveined
- 3 cups steamed white rice

Seafood Vegetable Pasta

1 cup chicken stock (page 149)

1 tablespoon extra virgin olive oil

2 ounces cleaned and peeled medium (36 to 40 count) shrimp

2 ounces cleaned and cooked crawfish tail meat

1/2 cup blanched broccoli florets

1/2 cup blanched carrot slices

1 tablespoon cornstarch

3 tablespoons water

1 pound cooked, drained pasta

1 tablespoon chopped fresh dill

Pinch of ground black pepper

Finely chopped green onions, for garnish

Serves 4

Every once in a while I try to lose a few pounds—and nearly every night at the restaurant, I end up cooking for somebody in the dining room who's trying. Despite the bad timing of such an effort any time you're in New Orleans, we've found that this lowfat shrimp and pasta dish does the bare minimum of damage to the waistline.

PUT the chicken stock in a small saucepan and bring to a boil. Set aside.

In a large nonstick pan, heat the olive oil and sauté the shrimp just until they turn pink, about 2 minutes. Stir in the crawfish, chicken stock, broccoli, and carrots and bring to a low boil.

In a small bowl, dissolve the cornstarch in the water and stir the mixture into the pan to thicken the liquid. Add the pasta to the sauce and toss. Sprinkle with the dill and season with the pepper. Sprinkle the green onions over the top and serve.

Pasta Genevieve

Serves 4

Seafood is tossed with pasta quite often these days, but this dish is a snippier, snappier departure from the norm. The highlights, besides fresh shrimp, are the flavors of the wilted spinach and balsamic vinegar.

TO prepare the bell peppers, grill over an open flame until charred on all sides and dip in ice water. Strip off and discard the charred outer skin, and seed, derib, and dice the peppers.

In a medium bowl, add the blackening seasoning and shrimp and toss to coat. In a large pan, sauté the garlic in the olive oil over medium heat until it starts to turn golden. Add the shrimp and cook, stirring, for 3 to 4 minutes, just until pink. Add the roasted peppers and the anchovies and sauté for 1 minute. Add the vinegar and pasta, and season to taste with black pepper. Sprinkle the cheese over the top and toss until the pasta is heated through. Stir in the spinach and cook just until it is wilted, 3 to 4 minutes. Serve immediately.

2 large red bell peppers

1 teaspoon blackening seasoning (page 145)

1 pound medium (36 to 40 count) shrimp, peeled and deveined

1 1/2 tablespoons chopped garlic

2 tablespoons extra virgin olive oil

4 anchovy fillets, mashed

2 tablespoons balsamic vinegar

1 pound cooked linguine

Freshly ground black pepper to taste

4 tablespoons freshly grated pecorino-romano cheese

2 cups chopped fresh spinach

Shrimp and Eggplant Casserole

Serves 6 to 8

2 eggplants, peeled and diced

¹/₂ cup butter

1 large onion, diced (1 cup)

4 ribs celery, diced (1 cup)

2 green bell peppers, diced

¹/₄ cup chopped fresh parsley

¹/₄ cup chopped garlic

1¹/₂ cups diced chicken

1¹/₂ cups small (50 to 60 count) shrimp, peeled and deveined

³/₄ tablespoon Italian seasoning (page 149)

1 tablespoon blackening seasoning (page 145)

1¹/₂ cups chicken stock (page 149)

1 teaspoon Worcestershire sauce

1 teaspoon Crystal hot sauce or other Louisiana hot sauce

¹/₂ cup finely chopped green onions

1 cup Italian-style bread crumbs

¹/₂ cup freshly grated Parmesan cheese

In some places, I'm told, casseroles are about as current as I Love Lucy. *Not so in New Orleans, where every dinner party arranged buffet-style features a mob scene around somebody's proprietary blend of seafood, eggplant, artichoke, and the like. This recipe reflects what the best of those party plates is all about, a delicious melting-pot marriage of Creole and Sicilian.*

BOIL the eggplants in salted water until tender, about 20 minutes, then drain and reserve.

Preheat the oven to 350 degrees.

Melt the butter in a large pan; add the onion, celery, bell peppers, parsley, and garlic and sauté until the vegetables start to become transparent, about 5 minutes. Add the eggplants and the remaining ingredients and stir to combine. Transfer the mixture to a casserole dish and bake for 20 to 25 minutes, until golden brown. Place the casserole in the middle of the table and let the folks dig in.

NOTE: This can be a main course, but it's also a great side for roasted chicken or pork.

Shrimp-Stuffed Mirlitons

Serves 6

There are several things New Orleans cooks love to do with mirlitons, a vegetable known as "chayote" in the Southwest, as "vegetable pears" in some other places, and by close to a dozen names across the Caribbean. Whatever you call the main ingredient (we pronounce it "mell-a-tawn"), it's the stuffing that really drives this dish home.

BOIL the mirlitons in salted water 20 to 25 minutes, or until tender, then remove them from the water and scoop out the meat, reserving both the meat and the "shell" for stuffing.

Preheat the oven to 350 degrees.

Melt the butter in a medium sauté pan; add the onions, celery, and bell peppers; and sauté until translucent. Add the ham, bay leaves, and shrimp, sautéing just until the shrimp turn pink. Add the bread and chicken stock and reduce over medium-high heat, 5 to 6 minutes. Add the remaining ingredients and reserved mirliton flesh, discarding seeds, and stir to mix thoroughly. Cook for 5 minutes, then remove from the heat to cool.

Using a spoon, stuff the mixture into the reserved mirliton shells and bake for 15 minutes. Serve each person 1 stuffed half mirliton.

NOTE: For best results in any stuffing with French bread, the bread should not be soggy. So after soaking the bread, place it in a colander at the sink and press out any remaining water with your hands.

3 mirlitons, halved along the visible vertical line

2 tablespoons butter

1/2 cup chopped onions

1/2 cup chopped celery

1/2 cup chopped green bell peppers

1 cup coarsely chopped ham

2 bay leaves

1 cup small (50 to 60 count) shrimp, peeled and deveined

1 1/2 cups cubed stale French bread, soaked in water and drained

1 1/2 cups chicken stock (page 149)

1/4 cup chopped green onions

1/4 cup chopped fresh parsley

2 teaspoons Worcestershire sauce

4 teaspoons Crystal hot sauce or other Louisiana hot sauce

1 teaspoon Italian seasoning (page 149)

2 teaspoons coarsely ground black pepper

1/2 teaspoon salt

1/2 cup Italian-style bread crumbs

WE are flying on the water, cutting across bay after bay, dipping though passes that flow like rivers with the tide, grabbing sudden lefts or rights as paths through the high, blowing grasses present themselves.

Our boatman smiles, revealing one gold tooth. Above the tooth, covering his head, is a red bandanna that flaps wildly in the wind. Below the tooth are a black Harley-Davidson T-shirt, cutoff jeans, and bare feet that seem stained with several varieties of petroleum products. I'm being chauffeured by Jean Lafitte's ghost, a pirate in search of the oysters in Louisiana waters.

Even among this city's many oyster fanatics, few care enough about the source or the process to visit oystermen in their native habitat, and, indeed, most oystermen are fervently in favor of keeping it that way. But I grew up around these people, and I met nearly all of the families back when my father ran his restaurant.

The oyster lugger finally appears on the horizon. The lugger, the heart and soul of Louisiana's century-old oyster industry, is more a factory than a boat. It is a ramshackle (though, of necessity, sturdy) construction of dark, stained wood, with a cabin for sleeping, frayed tarps hanging from every angle to provide shade, and plenty of greased chains to lower and raise the clawlike dredges that extract the oysters.

Many fishing fads have come and gone over the generations, some quite recently with devastating effect, but Louisiana continues to produce more oysters than any other state in the Union. This is as it should be, since we consume more oysters than any other state as well.

We are welcomed aboard the lugger by the men who work it. There is much shrugging around the shed, much staring down at sun-bleached oyster shells, and much swigging of beer to wash down reality and the breakfast of fried chicken. There really isn't much for a visitor to do. The work is hard, repetitive, and probably dangerous to anyone from the suburbs who tries to lend a hand. The dredge goes down; the dredge comes up. The oysters and other things living and dead are dumped onto a wooden table. The discards go back over the side, and the crusty oysters end up in burlap sacks.

We eat so many oysters, in fact, that Mother Nature can't keep up. Oysters must be carefully farmed and cultivated throughout our brackish bayous and salt marshes. Shallow water bottoms are leased by the state to oyster growers, who then seed their turf with "spat," an unromantic name for young oysters. These oysters are moved closer to the salty waters of the Gulf—a wonderful process that gives the bivalves their characteristic flavor. In all, a typical oyster is moved four or five times before it's ready for market. If you've ever run into an oyster that's flat, flabby, and tasteless, you've probably run into one that somebody hustled to market for quick cash before its time.

Finally, there's the matter of who does all this oystering in Louisiana waters. Tourists, of course, presume this is a traditional Creole occupation, or even better, the province of crusty Cajuns who scurry about among the oyster beds between their feverish fais-do-do's—street parties to which entire villages are invited.

The truth is, nearly all Louisiana oystermen hail from the Dalmatian region of the former Yugoslavia. These strong-willed natives of the coastal province surrounding Dubrovnik were farming bivalves by the bay. When their own oyster beds faltered in the late 1800s and they heard rumors of rich pickings in America, the men and women headed off to this strange new world.

There were good times and bad times along the bayous. Many modern oystering families still talk about the Great Depression, when all they had to eat was whatever oysters they could farm. Today's Croatian grandmothers could write whole cookbooks on oyster cuisine, since they were forced to feed their large families on their crop, breakfast, lunch, and dinner.

HALF-SHELL LIVING

Historians tell us that among the old Creoles, the oyster loaf was known in French as the "mediatrice," or peacemaker. Whenever a gentleman would have a spat with his wife (and in this case, "spat" didn't mean young oysters), he would bring her an oyster loaf (a hollowed-out loaf of French bread filled with fried oysters) in hopes of appeasement. Apparently, it worked a lot better than flowers or Godiva chocolates. If he was very lucky, she might even share her oyster loaf with him.

In a sense, all of this only brings us to the threshold of New Orleans's single most famous contribution to the world of oyster cookery. Since 1899, baked oyster dishes have grabbed a special place in our oyster-loving hearts, and they've never even hinted they might let go.

The method of topping fresh oysters with some mixture of seafoods, seasonings, and sauces and then baking them until they're crusty and brown has become a food category unto itself, miraculously sidestepping the predictable moans from purists that the topping disguises the real flavor.

In New Orleans, a baked oyster dish is its own flavor, with the oysters as the buried treasure that gives the taste a theme. Through it all, the valiant oyster has shown itself to have a sense of humor, tolerating a barrage of abuses in order to stumble on the occasional moment of glory.

The first such moment is easy enough to date. It was 1899 when Jules Alciatore, second-generation proprietor of Antoine's, found himself missing the escargots of his native France. In response to a no-doubt distressing snail shortage, he decided to bake some oysters on the half shell and serve them on a bed of rock salt to retain the heat. The finished product, probably held together by a roux and flavored with Herbsaint or Pernod, was so rich it struck Alciatore as being worthy of Rockefeller. Thus a dish—and a whole genre of cooking—was born.

The dishes begotten by Rockefeller are glorious to behold, and even more glorious to sample. A close relative in time and place is Oysters Bienville. These oysters are topped with a mixture of chopped shrimp and mushrooms.

At least two super-rustic variants pay homage to the often-parallel Croatian and Sicilian traditions of the local oyster. Charbroiled oysters at Drago's combine both traditions with butter-rich seasonings and lots of Parmesan and romano on top. Oysters Mosca at Mosca's is a festival of garlic and olive oil served in a piping-hot casserole rather than a half shell. Each generation seems to produce its own favorite baked oyster dishes, with only time deciding which become classics like Rockefeller and Bienville.

Cornmeal-Fried Oysters

1 cup cornmeal

$^1/_2$ teaspoon salt

$^1/_2$ teaspoon freshly ground black pepper

$^1/_2$ teaspoon ground red pepper

16 oysters, shucked

Vegetable oil for deep-frying

Serves 4

Some of my customers tell me they're amazed at how different each type of fried seafood is at my restaurant. Apparently, some restaurants offer fried seafood that all tastes the same because everything is cooked in the same way and in the same batter. The best New Orleans seafood cooks know that each type of seafood has its own best conditions. Fried oysters, for example, need maximum crunch. And since they're moist anyway, there's no need for a batter—a gentle roll in the cornmeal does the trick.

I N a large bowl, season the cornmeal with the salt and black and red peppers, and roll each oyster in the mixture until covered. Shake off any excess coating and fry until golden brown in 350-degree oil, about 2 minutes. (To test the temperature of the oil, put a pinch of the cornmeal in the hot oil. If it sizzles right away, it is ready.) Transfer to paper towels to drain and serve immediately with french fries.

N O T E : To make an oyster loaf, slice an 8-inch piece of French bread lengthwise. Butter both sides. Mound with fried oysters, squeeze the juice of $^1/_2$ lemon over the oysters, sprinkle with Crystal hot sauce, and cover with sliced dill pickles. Place the bread pieces back together and bake in a 400-degree oven until golden brown. Cut in half and serve.

Oyster Stew

Serves 6

Like many traditional Creole dishes, this simple stew is a terrific showcase for the primary flavor—fresh Gulf oysters. Though clam juice is okay, try to shuck your own oysters and use the water, which is known as "oyster liquor," from the shell; your stew will be the better for it.

MELT the butter in a saucepan over medium heat and add the oyster water or clam juice. Add the oysters and cook just until they curl, about 2 minutes. Add the remaining ingredients and stir to mix. Serve hot in deep bowls.

2 tablespoons butter

1/2 cup oyster water or clam juice

1 dozen raw oysters, shucked

1/4 teaspoon salt or to taste

1/2 teaspoon coarsely ground black pepper

1 cup milk

1/2 cup heavy whipping cream

1/2 teaspoon Tabasco sauce

1/2 teaspoon Worcestershire sauce

2 tablespoons chopped green onions

2 tablespoons chopped fresh parsley

Garlic Oysters

Serves 8

When I was growing up in New Orleans, the taste and scent of garlic were everywhere. Even in families without Sicilian sides, you met garlic coming and going. Here's a new way to marry garlic and oysters. And since both are supposed to be aphrodisiacs . . .

PUT the oysters and the remaining ingredients except the linguine in a large skillet over medium heat. Cover with a tight-fitting lid and cook until the oyster shells open. As the liquid reduces, uncover and add up to 1 cup of water. Remove the skillet from the heat and lift out the opened oysters with a slotted spoon. Let them cool slightly in a bowl, and, using a sharp knife, cut the oysters from their shells, retaining the meat and juices and discarding the shells.

　　Place the skillet on the heat and add the steamed oysters. Reduce the liquid over high heat until you have 3/4 to 1 cup. Add the cooked linguine to the pan, toss well, and serve immediately.

　　NOTE: Make sure that there's always at least 1/4 inch of liquid in the pot at all times. If the liquid cooks down, just add a little more water.

10 small oysters in the shell, scrubbed

Juice of 1 1/2 fresh lemons, rind reserved

2 bay leaves

1 cup white wine

2 tablespoons minced garlic

1/2 cup butter

2 tablespoons freshly ground black pepper

8 ounces cooked linguine

Oyster-Spinach Pie

Serves 8 to 10

Topping

1¹/₂ cups Italian-style bread crumbs

1 cup romano cheese

2 tablespoons unsalted butter

2 tablespoons unsalted butter, at room temperature

¹/₂ cup chopped onions

¹/₂ cup chopped celery

¹/₂ cup chopped green bell peppers

3 dozen oysters, shucked

1¹/₂ teaspoons salt

2 teaspoons freshly ground black pepper

1 cup heavy whipping cream

1 cup milk

8 ounces cream cheese, at room temperature

1¹/₂ teaspoons Tabasco sauce

2 cups chopped fresh spinach

1 cup pecorino-romano cheese

3 eggs, beaten

2 (10-inch) unbaked pie crusts (page 150)

When I was growing up I heard stories of the hardships endured by Croatian oystermen and their families during the Great Depression. They had absolutely no money to buy food—but they had lots of oysters. Although this fabulous Oyster-Spinach Pie is an upgrade from those "no money" days, it reflects how Louisianians have found many ways to enjoy our beloved bivalves.

T 0 prepare the topping, put the bread crumbs, cheese, and butter in a large bowl. Cut together with a knife, like a streusel topping.

Preheat the oven to 350 degrees.

Melt the butter in a large pan. Add the onions, celery, and green peppers and sauté over medium-high heat for 5 to 6 minutes, until the vegetables are soft. Add the oysters, salt, pepper, cream, and milk, and cook, stirring, for 3 minutes, just until the oysters curl. Blend in the cream cheese and Tabasco with a spoon, followed by the spinach, cheese, and eggs.

Divide the filling between the pie crusts and bake in the oven until set, about 25 minutes. Remove the pies from the oven and sprinkle with the topping, then return the pies to the oven for 35 minutes, just until brown. Let cool to set and serve.

Oyster-Bacon Quiche

Serves 6 to 8

That line from the 1970s that "real men don't eat quiche" must have applied only to those fancy and frilly versions of quiche that were chic for a day or two. As created by the French, and here given character by both oysters and crumbled bacon, this quiche is likely to please both men and women, no matter how "real" they happen to be.

PREHEAT the oven to 350 degrees.

In a large pan over medium heat, sauté the bacon until crisp, then drain on paper towels and crumble it.

In a medium bowl, combine the bacon and the poached oysters. Reserve ¹/₂ cup of the oyster water. In a separate medium bowl, whisk together the eggs, cream, milk, flour, cheese, salt, pepper, Tabasco, and the reserved ¹/₂ cup oyster water. Blend the oyster-bacon mixture into the egg mixture and pour into the pie shell. Bake in the oven until set, about 25 minutes. Allow to cool. Slice into wedges and serve.

8 slices bacon

24 oysters, poached in their own water

4 eggs

¹/₂ cup heavy whipping cream

1 cup milk

1 tablespoon all-purpose flour

1¹/₂ cups grated Cheddar cheese

1 teaspoon salt

1 teaspoon freshly ground black pepper

1 teaspoon Tabasco sauce

1 (10-inch) unbaked pie crust (page 150)

How to Open an Oyster

For the uninitiated, prying open an oyster may be one of the most dangerous things you do in your life, an act of folly just this side of running with the bulls in Spain. But with practice and plenty of care, the business can be safe and satisfying.

You might start by watching a professional at one of New Orleans's many terrific oyster bars. The pros usually use a heavy lead anvil shaped like an "S" to hold the shell in place and an oyster knife, a tool that is notable for the fact that nuclear attack probably couldn't break off its blade. You don't need these tools to get the job done, but whatever tools you use, you need to be careful to avoid giving yourself quite a deep cut.

Using an oyster knife (or a strong screwdriver, if you don't have an official knife) and a paring knife on the side, or even one of those old-fashioned beer can openers that form a triangular hole, lay the oyster flat and steady it with one hand. Pry the shell open at the hinge, using the strong blade. You don't have to open the shell much, since you can slip in the small paring knife and sever the adductor muscle that connects to the top of the shell. Once the muscle is cut, the top shell should lift right off.

Next, slip the paring knife under the oyster itself and cut the second half of the muscle, allowing the juicy bivalve to nestle freely. You should leave the oyster on the deeper half of the shell, giving it a bed off of which it's unlikely to slide. And be sure to preserve every drop of the liquid inside the shell, the "oyster water" or "oyster liquid." Once you're skilled enough, you can open oysters over a pot to help with collecting all of the juices.

Most of all, be very careful with the knife. Even the pros hurt themselves badly from time to time.

Final bits of housekeeping include using your paring knife to scrape off any bitter-tasting dark mud that has lodged where the hinges had joined and also looking for any tiny pieces of shell that may be left on the oyster. These chips are so hard, seemingly prehistoric in their formation, that in any contest with the human tooth you can be sure the shell will win.

Sauce

1/4 cup Crystal hot sauce
or other Louisiana hot
sauce

1/4 cup honey

1/4 cup loosely packed
dark brown sugar

1 teaspoon orange zest

1 teaspoon lemon zest

Vegetable oil for deep-
frying

Coating

1 cup all-purpose flour

1 teaspoon salt

1 teaspoon freshly
ground black pepper

1/2 teaspoon garlic
powder

24 oysters, shucked

Barbecued Oysters

Serves 6 to 8

*As with our Barbecued Shrimp (page 40), our use of the word "bar-
becue" for this dish is quirky at best. My guess is that we're blending
some aspects of barbecue sauce with some aspects of buffalo wing
sauce. But, whatever we're up to, this is one of the best renditions of
oysters you're likely to find anywhere.*

T O prepare the sauce, whisk together all of the ingredients over
medium heat in a saucepan for 1 minute, or until the brown sugar
is dissolved and hot. Remove the sauce from the heat and let cool
at room temperature for at least 2 hours, or preferably overnight,
to allow the flavors to mingle.

Reheat the sauce in a skillet over medium heat. Heat the oil
to 350 degrees. While the oil is heating, mix together all of the
ingredients for the coating. Dredge the oysters in the coating, add
them to the hot oil, and deep-fry until golden brown, about 2
minutes.

To serve, place the oysters in a large serving bowl. Serve the
sauce in a separate bowl on the side for dipping, or lightly toss the
oysters in the sauce.

N O T E : When preparing the zest of a citrus fruit, grate only
the skin, not the bitter white pith. Zesting can be done with an
official "zester," or with a vegetable peeler or paring knife.

Oysters Bordelaise

Serves 6 to 8

Around New Orleans, the word "Bordelaise" doesn't refer as much to the style of Bordeaux as it does to garlic, pure and simple. Combining the simplest coating with freshly shucked oysters and then covering them with a sauce built atop our garlic butter—well, I don't see any way the people of Bordeaux wouldn't approve.

T0 prepare the sauce, sauté the garlic in the olive oil over medium-high heat for 1 to 2 minutes, and add the red pepper and parsley. Stir in the garlic butter and keep the sauce warm.

Dredge the oysters in the coating and deep-fry at 350 degrees until golden, about 2 minutes. Toss the fried oysters in the sauce and serve.

Sauce

1 teaspoon chopped garlic

1 tablespoon extra virgin olive oil

1/8 teaspoon crushed red pepper

1 teaspoon chopped fresh parsley

1 tablespoon garlic butter (page 146)

1 1/4 cups seasoned flour (page 145)

24 oysters, shucked

Vegetable oil for deep-frying

Oysters Rockefeller

12 to 15 oysters on the half shell

1/2 cup water

1 teaspoon salt

Rockefeller Sauce

2 tablespoons butter

1 cup chopped fresh spinach

1 cup chopped turnip greens

1 cup chopped green onions

1 cup chopped green bell peppers

1 cup chopped celery

1 cup chopped white onion

1 cup chopped parsley

1 tablespoon chopped garlic

2 cups oyster water, reserved from shucking

1 cup shucked oysters

1 teaspoon lemon zest

1 teaspoon Tabasco sauce

1 teaspoon salt

2 teaspoons coarsely ground black pepper

2 tablespoons Pernod

2/3 cup freshly grated pecorino-romano cheese

4 lemon wedges, as garnish

Serves 4

You may know the story: Oysters Rockefeller was invented early in this century by the good folks at Antoine's Restaurant, in the French Quarter, who declared the topping "rich enough for Rockefeller"— meaning, of course, millionaire John D. Now, every restaurant has its version, some more satisfying than others. I like to poach the oysters for just a minute or two before assembling the dish for baking.

P L A C E the oysters in the water with the salt, simmer over medium heat until the edges start to curl, then remove with a slotted spoon. Discard the poaching liquid.

To prepare the sauce, melt the butter in a large pan. Add the vegetables, parsley, and garlic, and sauté until the vegetables are soft and translucent, 8 to 10 minutes. Add the oyster water, oysters, and lemon zest, reducing over medium heat until the liquid is almost gone, about 6 minutes. Add the remaining ingredients for the sauce and transfer to a blender. Blend to form a smooth paste.

Preheat the oven to 400 degrees.

Spoon the oyster mixture over the oysters on the half shell, molding with hands. Set the oysters on a baking sheet and bake until the tops start to bubble and brown, about 5 minutes. Set on small plates, 3 or 4 oysters per person. Serve with lemon wedges.

N O T E : This recipe makes about 8 cups of Rockefeller sauce. If you have leftover sauce, use it for Oyster Andouille Pasta (page 63). You'll love it.

Oyster Andouille Pasta

Serves 4

Once you've made and eaten Oysters Rockefeller, there are still some uses for any leftover sauce. Here is one, a pasta dish that adds fresh spinach to the flavor profile of the renowned baked oyster dish.

MELT the butter in a large pan over medium heat; add the andouille, shucked oysters, and oyster water; and sauté over medium heat, reducing the liquid until it is almost gone, about 4 minutes. Stir in the spinach, Rockefeller sauce, and cream and cook just to heat through. Season with the salt and pepper, add the pasta, and toss in the pan until the pasta is heated through. Serve on plates and top with the cheese.

1 tablespoon unsalted butter

2 ounces andouille sausage, cut in thin slices

1 dozen oysters, shucked

1/2 cup oyster water or clam juice

1 cup loosely packed fresh spinach

1/2 cup Rockefeller sauce (page 62)

1 cup heavy whipping cream

1/4 teaspoon salt

1/4 teaspoon freshly ground black pepper

8 ounces linguine, cooked

1/4 cup freshly grated pecorino-romano cheese

Open-Faced Oyster Sandwiches with Blue Cheese Crumble

Serves 4

4 strips bacon

Sauce

1 tablespoon melted butter

½ cup blue cheese, plus extra for topping

½ cup heavy whipping cream

1½ teaspoons chopped fresh parsley

½ teaspoon Tabasco sauce

1 tablespoon olive oil

1 cup fresh spinach

4 large slices fresh bread, toasted

16 Cornmeal-Fried Oysters (page 54)

This is a newer creation of ours, and you should have been there in the kitchen when we all tasted it for the first time. As often happens in our recipes, we take something familiar—in this case, fried oysters—and carry them someplace they've never been before.

IN a large pan over medium heat, sauté the bacon until crisp, drain on paper towels, and crumble it. Set aside.

In a medium saucepan, add all of the ingredients for the sauce. Whisk the mixture together over medium heat until it boils. Remove from the heat.

In a small saucepan, heat the olive oil and sauté the spinach just until it starts to wilt, 3 to 4 minutes. Remove the pan from the heat.

To assemble, place the spinach on the toasted bread on 4 small plates. Top with some of the oysters, spoon some of the sauce over the oysters and bread, and sprinkle some of the bacon and blue cheese over the sauce. Serve immediately.

Oyster Patties

Serves 8

It's hard to think of "party food" in New Orleans without thinking of oyster patties. The disappointment in the air is palpable if somebody throws a party without these. Here's a safe bet to make your parties memorable.

MAKE a light blond roux by combining the butter and flour and place in a large bowl. Add the oyster water, cayenne pepper, salt, and black pepper to form a broth. Set aside. Poach the oysters, onions, mushrooms, and parsley until the sides of the oysters curl, 1 to 2 minutes. Place the mixture in a blender and purée. Add the mixture to the broth. Add the milk, cream, and Tabasco and stir to combine.

Preheat the oven to 350 degrees.

Cut the sheet of pastry dough into 8 squares. Pinch corners of the dough to form baskets and bake until golden brown and puffed. When ready to serve, spoon the hot oyster mixture into the pastry shells and serve immediately.

$1/2$ cup melted butter

$1/2$ cup all-purpose flour

4 cups oyster water or clam juice

Pinch of cayenne pepper

$1/2$ teaspoon salt

$1/2$ teaspoon freshly ground black pepper

24 oysters, shucked

$1/2$ cup chopped onions

$1/2$ cup chopped button mushrooms

2 tablespoons chopped fresh parsley

1 cup milk

1 cup heavy whipping cream

Dash of Tabasco sauce

1 sheet puff pastry dough

WHEN I was little, I used to go crabbing with a guy named Glen Guillot. Mr. Glen, as I called him, had a "putt-putt" boat, just a little skiff with a Briggs and Stratton lawnmower-style motor on it. It didn't go too fast. That boat was as crusty as some of the crabs we caught. Mr. Glen was crusty, too. His face was tanned and wrinkled, and he had a dramatically receding hairline. When Mr. Glen would get back from each trip, he'd sit in the bar for 30 minutes or so and just talk. He spoke with that down-the-road, fishing village accent while he drank his beer. The beer was important to him. Then he'd go out and run his crab line again.

Mr. Glen ran what he called a "palanga." You tied a cork and a heavy weight to one end of the line and a cork in front of the weight so you could pick the line up. You placed it over a steel rim that hung over the edge of the boat and putt-putted along in your boat with something like a wire net that acted like a bat. As you picked the line up, you'd find the crabs were holding onto the bait, usually chicken necks. You had to bat them into the boat. Once the crabs were in the boat you had to scramble because they would try to bite you. It got pretty interesting, but that's how we would do it.

Mr. Glen had to have his six-pack with him when he ran the line, because that was part of it. He had this bottle called a Little Joe, a miniature longneck, long before the Miller ponies ever came out.

Another time, we used a simplified version: just a scoop net and a string with a chicken neck tied to it. Wherever my father would be buying crab or shrimp down there by Delacroix Island or Hopedale or Yscloskey, we'd sit on the dock, my brother and I, and we'd throw our chicken neck overboard. We'd let it go to the bottom and let it sit for a while, and then we'd gently and slowly pull it up. If there was a crab hanging on it, we'd scoop it up in the net and have fresh crabs.

This was the old way of crabbing. In the modern way, you put the bait in a trap and it's unattended. With the palanga, you went and ran that line every 30 minutes until the crabs ate all the bait.

For a while I was going into Lake Borgne and running crab traps professionally. For that, with my cousin Sonny, we used to run maybe 300 to 400 traps. I remember it was so still on Lake Borgne, not a ripple on the water, and it was hot, hot, hot, with the sun beating down. I'd look out over the horizon and say, "Sonny, how many more traps are there?" and he'd say, "Just what you can see." I never realized you could only see eight or ten before the horizon would take them out of sight. It would take us four or five hours to stop at every trap. Of course, my relatives fished around the clock.

Crab Stew

Serves 8

To me, this dish is about going to the fish camp. It's rich, it's full of flavor, and it uses what most folks I grew up around could find at their fish camp—whether they lived there full-time, all summer long, or only on weekends. This is mostly a country Cajun dish, and definitely not New Orleans Sicilian. My mother always made her crab stew with red gravy, and I was pretty much grown before I tasted this version cooked by a friend, Larry Thibodeaux. Well, I never vote against my mother's version of anything, but I do promise you, this is terrific.

COMBINE the $^1/_3$ cup flour and $^2/_3$ cup water in a bowl. Set aside.

Prepare a dark roux by heating the margarine in a heavy skillet over medium heat. Whisk in the $^1/_4$ cup flour. Cook, stirring constantly, until dark brown, 8 to 10 minutes. The roux should be the color of coffee grounds. Remove from the heat but continue to stir. Set aside.

Melt the butter in a large saucepan over medium heat; add the onions and cook, stirring constantly, until the onions caramelize, about 3 minutes. Add the celery and bell peppers, and cook for 3 minutes. Add the dark roux, stir until incorporated, and add the sherry. Cook for 2 minutes and add the stock. Add the crabs, bay leaves, hot sauce, crab boil, and black pepper; increase the heat; and bring the mixture to a boil.

Stir the flour and water mixture and add it to the stew. Boil for 3 minutes, then decrease the heat and simmer uncovered for 45 minutes. Remove the bay leaves, stir in the green onions, and serve over steamed white rice.

$^1/_3$ cup plus $^1/_4$ cup all-purpose flour

$^2/_3$ cup water

$^1/_4$ cup margarine

1 cup unsalted butter

1 cup chopped onions

1 cup chopped celery

1 cup chopped green bell peppers

$^1/_2$ cup dry sherry

3 quarts fish or chicken stock (pages 148 and 149)

3 pounds crabs, broken in pieces

3 bay leaves

$^1/_3$ cup Crystal hot sauce or Louisiana hot sauce

$^1/_2$ teaspoon liquid crab boil

1 tablespoon cracked black pepper

$^1/_2$ cup chopped green onions

4 cups steamed white rice

Crab Cakes

Serves 6

½ cup unsalted butter

1 cup chopped onions

1 cup chopped green bell peppers

1 cup chopped celery

3 bay leaves

1 loaf French bread, cubed, soaked in water, and drained

2 cups fish or chicken stock (pages 148 and 149)

2 teaspoons Italian seasoning (page 149)

2 teaspoons cracked black pepper

2 teaspoons Tabasco sauce

3 teaspoons hot sauce

1 teaspoon Worcestershire sauce

1 pound crabmeat, picked clean of any shell fragments

½ cup chopped green onions

Salt

2 cups Italian-style bread crumbs

1 tablespoon olive oil

Creamy crab sauce (page 147)

When I was growing up, nobody had ever heard of a crab cake. We didn't know they would someday be a best-seller on almost every restaurant menu, including ours. But New Orleans did have several types of "prehistoric" crab cakes. One was the New Orleans famous stuffed crab, made with a savory crab stuffing that was pressed into a cleaned crab shell. We also made something called a crab chop, using the same stuffing we used for the stuffed crab but formed into a cake and grilled with a little oil. Funny how the same stuffing came out completely different depending on how you cooked it. So, you might say that even though for many years we didn't get to enjoy crab cakes as tasty as the ones in this recipe, we had plenty of practice.

MELT the butter in a medium saucepan over medium heat and stir in the onions, bell peppers, celery, and bay leaves. Cook until the vegetables are soft, about 5 minutes, and then add the bread and cook, stirring constantly, for 1 minute. Add the stock, Italian seasoning, black pepper, Tabasco, hot sauce, and Worcestershire sauce and cook until the mixture thickens, about 5 minutes. Gently add the crabmeat and heat thoroughly, but don't overcook, about 3 minutes. Add the green onions and salt to taste and remove from the heat. Remove the bay leaves and discard. Let cool.

Preheat the oven to 400 degrees.

To prepare the crab cakes, scoop the mixture into balls and roll in the bread crumbs. Form into 12 cakes about ½ inch thick and 3 inches wide. Coat the bottom of a baking sheet with the olive oil and set the crab cakes on the pan. Bake in the oven for 10 to 15 minutes, or until golden brown. Serve immediately. Top with 1 tablespoon of creamy crab sauce per cake. Serve immediately.

NOTE: These cakes are essentially a universal crab stuffing, perfect for chicken, fish, or pork. Be creative!

Crab-Stuffed Avocado

Serves 8 as an appetizer; serves 4 as an entrée

This is a light, summery dish with its own fresh salsa. If you want to be more old New Orleans, just use the remoulade sauce from Shrimp Remoulade (page 28).

CUT the avocados in half and remove and discard the pit. Sprinkle the avocado with the lime juice and place the halves on a bed of shredded lettuce on each plate.

In a bowl, combine the stuffing ingredients. Press ¼ cup of the crabmeat stuffing into each avocado half.

To prepare the salsa, combine all of the ingredients for the salsa in a blender. Spoon the salsa over the stuffed avocados and serve.

4 ripe avocados, chilled

Freshly squeezed lime juice

4 cups shredded iceberg lettuce

Stuffing

½ pound crabmeat, picked clean of any shell fragments

3 tablespoons chopped celery

2 tablespoons chopped green onions

¼ teaspoon Tabasco sauce

½ teaspoon Worcestershire sauce

4 tablespoons mayonnaise

¼ tablespoon salt

1 tablespoon freshly squeezed lemon juice

Fiesta Salsa

2 jalapeños, thinly sliced

2 tablespoons olive oil

2 tablespoons chopped green onions

1 teaspoon chopped garlic

1 tablespoon chopped cilantro

1 10-ounce can tomatoes

1 teaspoon salt

Crab Mold

Serves 8

8 ounces cream cheese, at room temperature

1/2 cup sour cream

2 tablespoons chopped green onions

1/4 teaspoon Tabasco sauce

1/2 teaspoon salt

1/4 pound crab claw meat

Molds may not be common at parties anymore, but this mold, made with crabmeat, is sure to become a party favorite. Best of all, the recipe works great with almost any seafood, particularly with crawfish, shrimp, small smoked oysters, or diced smoked salmon.

IN a bowl, using an electric mixer, whip all of the ingredients together thoroughly. Pack the mixture into a bowl or ring mold. Refrigerate for at least 2 hours. Serve chilled with crackers.

Crabmeat Martin

Serves 4

1 pound crabmeat, picked clean of any shell fragments

2 tablespoons Creole mustard

2 tablespoons finely chopped green onions

Topping

1 cup mayonnaise

2 tablespoons yellow mustard

1/2 teaspoon Tabasco sauce

1/2 tablespoon Worcestershire sauce

Joe Martin was both a hero and a mentor to me. He was an old-fashioned New Orleans kitchen guy who never had national fame as a chef, but he could cook better than a lot of household names. Not only that, he was a great teacher, developing an army of everyday workers who were the backbone of good food served all over town. The funny thing is, for all the people he taught, he never wrote down his best dishes. He used to make this one hunched over like it was a big secret. I pieced the recipe together from some of the guys he taught. Joe, if you're looking down on this dish from someplace where the work isn't so hard, I hope you don't think we're leaving something out!

PREHEAT the oven to 350 degrees.

Gently toss the crabmeat with the mustard and green onions in a bowl, being careful not to break up the crabmeat. Divide the mixture between 4 ramekins. Using an electric mixer, whip together the topping ingredients in a mixing bowl and spread the topping on the crabmeat mixture. Bake in the oven until thoroughly heated and the sauce is golden brown and bubbly, about 8 minutes. Serve hot.

Crab Toast

Serves 8 to 10 as an appetizer

For a spectacular party appetizer, try this upgraded version of the traditional garlic bread. It's mostly about crabmeat, of course, but it packs a lot of not-so-subtle flavors as well.

PREHEAT the oven to 350 degrees.

Melt the cream cheese in a saucepan over medium heat. Place the garlic powder and chardonnay in a medium bowl and add the melted cream cheese, stirring to combine. Add the green onions, pepper, and Worcestershire and Tabasco sauces and stir well. Cook over medium heat just until heated through, about 2 minutes. Stir in the blackening seasoning, lemon zest and juice, and Creole mustard. Remove the pan from the heat and gently stir in the crabmeat.

Spread the mixture across the open face of the bread and sprinkle generously with the cheese. Place the bread on a baking sheet and bake in the oven until the top is golden and bubbling, 7 to 8 minutes. Remove the bread from the oven, slice it on the diagonal into 1-inch nibbles, and serve hot.

8 ounces cream cheese

1 tablespoon garlic powder

¼ cup chardonnay

¼ cup chopped green onions

½ teaspoon coarsely ground black pepper

½ teaspoon Worcestershire sauce

¼ teaspoon Tabasco sauce

¼ teaspoon blackening seasoning (page 145)

¼ teaspoon grated lemon zest

1 teaspoon freshly squeezed lemon juice

1 teaspoon Creole mustard

½ pound crabmeat, picked clean of any shell fragments

1 loaf French bread, sliced lengthwise

1 cup grated Cheddar cheese

How to Crack a Crab

As with crawfish, there's a city full of wisdom on how to get into a boiled crab. Most of it turns on how much good stuff you wish to eat. Locals discard nothing that's good to eat, no matter what it looks like or feels like on the tongue. And besides, it's pretty hard to argue with 300 years of survival.

Opening a boiled crab isn't rocket science, but it does require some practice. In other words, you can get enough to eat the first time out, but you may miss a lot and you won't set any speed records while you're at it. Start by simply lifting a boiled crab in the palm of one hand and placing your other hand over the top. Close your hand firmly on the shell points and lift off the top of the shell. At this stage, you can gaze down inside the body and, using a handy knife, scrape away the "dead man," or gills, along with the gizzard behind the eyes. While you're at it, get rid of the mouth at the front and the "apron" at the back. (This confirms that we in New Orleans won't really eat *anything*.)

The crab claws are obvious places to begin to eat. Crack them open with the back of a knife or with a small nutcracker and enjoy every bit of the sweet meat. Next, break the body into halves and use the legs as handles to crack the halves into segments. Every crack should produce a handle with a lump of meat sticking out of it. Clearly, Mother Nature has been kind enough to give us not only the delicacy but also the silverware.

The prize in all of this are the large, delicate lumps attached to the flippers in back. These are picked commercially and sold as lump crabmeat for seafood cocktails and for a high-class, high-priced garnish. But don't obsess over these: you'll probably be just as happy with the tiny bits of meat you can suck out of each tiny crab leg. The goal, as always, is to leave little or nothing wonderful behind.

Hot Chile Crab Claws

Serves 4 as an appetizer

I love the flavors the Vietnamese have brought to New Orleans, and their hardworking approach to life has served them well in this hot, steamy river delta that's so much like the area many of them left behind. While I don't make it to their open-air markets as much as I'd like, I do think of them every time I make this dish.

COMBINE the ingredients for the sauce in a sauté pan or wok over medium-high heat, stirring, for 1 or 2 minutes, or until the flavors combine. Add the crab claws and toss to heat them through. Garnish with the cilantro and serve immediately.

Marinated Chilled Crab Claws with Salsa

Serves 4 as an appetizer

If you want a cooling dish for a hot day or evening, toss together this Latin-influenced favorite of mine. It's like a gazpacho that stops short of being a soup. I like these crab claws served over a bed of shredded lettuce, but they could probably find a happy bed almost anywhere.

IN a large bowl, mix together all of the ingredients for the salsa. Add the crab claws to the bowl and marinate in the refrigerator for 4 to 6 hours. Serve over shredded lettuce.

Hot Chile Sauce

2 tablespoons sesame oil

4 tablespoons chopped green onions

2 tablespoons chopped garlic

4 tablespoons chile paste

2 teaspoons Asian fish sauce

1/2 cup sherry

1 pound crab claws

1 teaspoon chopped cilantro, for garnish

Salsa

2 cups chopped fresh tomatoes

4 tablespoons chopped green onions

2 teaspoons chopped garlic

2 teaspoons chopped fresh cilantro

2 tablespoons freshly squeezed lemon juice

2 tablespoons coarsely ground black pepper

2 tablespoons chopped jalapeño

2 cups Bloody Mary mix

1 pound crab claws

1 head iceberg lettuce, shredded

Rhoda's Crab Fingers

1 cup butter, melted

1/2 tablespoon olive oil

2 tablespoons chopped garlic

1/2 tablespoon chopped green onions

1/2 tablespoon chopped fresh parsley

1 pound crab claws

1 teaspoon coarsely ground black pepper

1/2 teaspoon Italian seasoning (page 149)

1 cup Italian-style bread crumbs

4 slices lemon, cut 1/4 inch thick

Serves 4

If you value great taste more than neatness, or if you just don't mind going through lots of napkins, you'll love this vaguely Sicilian, totally New Orleans creation named after my fiancée. It's drippy, and it involves eating the meat off each crab claw—preferably after sopping up more garlicky bread crumbs.

PREHEAT the oven to 350 degrees.

In a large sauté pan over medium-high heat, heat the butter with the olive oil and stir in the garlic, green onions, and parsley. Carefully add the crab claws and the remaining ingredients. Place in an ovenproof casserole dish and bake in the oven for 5 minutes, or until the top is golden brown. Serve immediately.

Crabmeat-Stuffed Jalapeños

Serves 6

In 1948, the same year my dad opened his seafood restaurant on Elysian Fields, the city's first Mexican restaurant opened next door. My dad used to send me running to El Ranchito every now and then for a Mexican treat, a couple of hot tamales. El Ranchito is every bit as gone as my family's restaurant, but I think of it and its tastes and smells every time I make a dish like this. Don't worry about the "Italian-style" bread crumbs; the oregano and other herbs fit right into the Latin flavor profile, providing a variation that helps melting pots like New Orleans start melting in the first place.

IN a large bowl, mix together all of the ingredients for the stuffing. Generously stuff the jalapeños, molding the crabmeat mixture into a ball. Put the flour and bread crumbs into separate bowls.

To make the whitewash, in a medium bowl, use a whisk to beat together the egg, milk, and flour until incorporated and smooth. Dip the jalapeños first into the seasoned flour, then into the whitewash, and finally, into the bread crumbs. Discard the remaining flour, whitewash, and bread crumbs.

Heat the vegetable oil to 350 degrees in a deep-fryer and fry the stuffed jalapeños (in batches, to avoid crowding) until they are golden brown, about 2 minutes. Drain on paper towels. Serve immediately on a platter.

Stuffing

1/2 pound crabmeat, picked clean of any shell fragments

1/2 cup Cheddar cheese

4 ounces cream cheese, at room temperature

1 tablespoon finely chopped cilantro

1 teaspoon minced garlic

1/2 teaspoon salt

1/2 teaspoon ground cumin

36 whole jalapeños, sliced lengthwise

1/2 cup seasoned flour (page 145)

1/2 cup Italian-style bread crumbs

Whitewash

1 egg

2 cups milk

1/4 cup seasoned flour (page 145)

Vegetable oil for deep-frying

Garlic Crab Claws

Serves 2 to 4

½ cup white wine

½ cup garlic butter (page 146)

1 tablespoon Worcestershire sauce

¼ teaspoon Tabasco sauce

½ pound crab claws

¼ teaspoon blackening seasoning (page 145)

Here's another of those quick classics I picked up from my mentor, Joe Martin. Joe actually used to bake the dish with similar results, but I find that most people prefer the claws sautéed these days. The big deal, after all, is the garlic butter, which is good on almost anything. Serve this with plenty of crusty French bread.

POUR the wine into a medium saucepan over medium-high heat and reduce the liquid by about half, 3 to 4 minutes. Stir in the garlic butter, Worcestershire sauce, and Tabasco sauce and stir until the butter is melted. Add the crab claws and toss until they are coated and warm, about 2 minutes. Sprinkle the seasoning over the crab. Serve hot.

Fried Crab Fingers

Serves 6

Crab fingers are the bottom half of the claw with crabmeat sticking out. Simple, casual, wonderful—I could just sit around all night and nibble on these babies. The crabmeat is so clean and sweet, and the bread crumbs are so fragrant. These crab fingers are good all by themselves, but I always eat them with cocktail sauce.

MEASURE out and set aside ¹/₂ cup of the seasoned flour. Use the remaining flour to dust the crab fingers, shaking off any excess. In a large bowl, combine the reserved flour with the bread crumbs.

To prepare the whitewash, in a medium bowl, use a whisk to beat together the egg, milk, and flour until incorporated and smooth. Dip the crab into the whitewash and roll until well coated. Discard the remaining whitewash.

Fry in a deep-fryer in oil preheated to 350 degrees until golden brown, 1 to 2 minutes. Drain on paper towels and serve with cocktail sauce.

²/₃ cup seasoned flour (page 145)

2 pounds crab fingers

¹/₂ cup Italian-style bread crumbs

Whitewash

1 egg

2 cups milk

¹/₄ cup seasoned flour (page 145)

Vegetable oil for deep-frying

Cocktail sauce (page 146)

Stone Crabs with Creole Dipping Sauce

Dipping Sauce

1/2 cup mayonnaise

1 tablespoon Creole mustard

1 tablespoon freshly squeezed lime juice

1 tablespoon chopped cilantro

1 tablespoon prepared horseradish

1/4 teaspoon grated lime zest

1/8 teaspoon salt

1/2 teaspoon Cointreau

24 cracked stone (or other large) crab claws, cooked and chilled

Serves 4 to 6

Everybody seems to think of stone crabs as belonging to Miami Beach, but the truth is, we've always had them here in Louisiana; it's just that for a long time, we didn't try eating them. When I was a kid, stone crabs would sometimes come up in a net or a trap. We thought they were monsters from the deep. Once, when my Uncle George ate a stone crab claw, I waited for him to fall over dead. Uncle George was fine, and so are our very own Louisiana stone crabs.

I N a blender, blend together all of the ingredients for the sauce until well incorporated and the mixture is smooth. Serve in a bowl with the crab claws in a separate bowl.

SOFTSHELL CRABS

My family used to visit a couple who lived in Mandeville, Louisiana, right off the beach. Pelligrin was their name. They lived back in the quiet days of Mandeville. Every morning, they'd hunt for green softshell crabs and place them in boxes that were staked in Lake Pontchartrain. In those days, the boxes were big with slots on the bottom just large enough to let the fresh water in but not enough to let the crab out. There was a trapdoor on the top. The Pelligrins would go over the concrete steps that led down to the water's edge and wade into the lake to check on the crabs. When softshell crabs decide to come out of the shell, you only have one or two hours before their shells start to harden.

When the Pelligrins had a lot of crabs in their boxes, they'd fish around the clock. He would go, and then she would go, every couple of hours, day and night. They'd take the softshell crabs out and get them ready, and my father would go and buy them for the restaurant.

There are some good things you can do with frozen softshell crabs, including sautéing and deep-frying them, but when you're lucky enough to have fresh softshells, as we do so often in southern Louisiana, I don't think there's a better flavor than simply broiling them. I know, you've probably learned to eat these delicate crabs some other way. But don't try them your way again until you've tried them my way. They're so flavorful, so different from anything you've tried before.

Lemon-Broiled Softshell Crab

4 fresh softshell crabs, cleaned

1 lemon, cut in half

Salt and black pepper, to taste

4 to 6 tablespoons butter, melted

Serves 4

I don't apologize for loving fried softshell crabs, or for selling them by the truckload at my restaurant. But I do believe that if you have perfect, kicking-fresh softshells, you just might like them better broiled than any other way. And once you have such a treat set in front of you, don't disguise it with much of anything.

PREHEAT the broiler to 400 degrees.

Set the cleaned softshells, belly side up, on a baking sheet and pour about $1/4$ inch of water into the pan. Squeeze the lemon halves over the crabs and into the liquid, setting the squeezed lemon on the pan. Season the crabs to taste with salt and pepper.

Set the pan under the broiler and cook until the legs curl up and the outside turns golden brown, about 10 minutes. Transfer to dinner plates and spoon some of the melted butter over the top. Serve immediately.

Fried Softshell Crab

Whitewash

1 egg

2 cups milk

$1/4$ cup seasoned flour (page 145)

$1/2$ cup seasoned flour (page 145)

$2/3$ cup seasoned cornmeal (page 97)

4 softshell crabs

Vegetable oil for deep-frying

Serves 4

Here you go—a true New Orleans favorite. You'll spot fried softshells almost everywhere, from the fancy places that serve creamy pasta alongside them to the absolute dives that put them on French bread for one of the world's best po-boys. Fried softshells get the locals excited any way they are served.

TO prepare the whitewash, in a medium bowl, use a whisk to beat together the egg, milk, and flour until incorporated and smooth.

Put the flour and cornmeal into separate bowls. Dust each softshell crab with the seasoned flour and dip it in the whitewash. Dredge the crab in the cornmeal, shaking off any excess. Deep-fry one at a time in a fryer with the oil preheated to 350 degrees, until the crab floats and is golden brown, 2 to 3 minutes. Drain on paper towels and serve immediately.

Marinated Softshell Crab with Blue Cheese Crumbles

Serves 4

You know me, I'll get creative with anything if I stare at it long enough. After all these years of broiling and frying softshell crabs, I suddenly got rolling on something a little different. I bet you'll like the way these marinated and sautéed softshells taste atop some bouncy, barely wilted greens with a few crumbles of pungent blue cheese here and there.

IN a mixing bowl, combine the lemon juice, honey, and hot sauce. Place the softshell crabs in the marinade and refrigerate for about 30 minutes.

In a small bowl, whisk together the horseradish and vinegar and set aside.

Place a skillet over medium heat and melt the unsalted butter. Remove the crabs from the marinade, reserving the liquid. Sprinkle the crabs with the flour and shake off any excess. Sauté the softshells in the hot butter for about $1^1/_2$ minutes per side, until golden brown. Drain on paper towels.

In a large bowl, toss the greens with the horseradish-vinegar mixture. Divide over 4 dinner plates and season to taste with salt and black pepper.

Place the skillet back over medium heat and pour in the white wine, scraping to release the browned bits from the bottom. Add the reserved marinade and reduce by half, cooking for about 2 minutes. Swirl in the cold butter to enrich the sauce.

Place a softshell crab on the mixed greens and spoon some of the sauce over the top. Sprinkle the blue cheese over the crabs and the greens, and serve.

2 tablespoons freshly squeezed lemon juice

2 tablespoons honey

2 tablespoons Crystal hot sauce or other Louisiana hot sauce

4 fresh softshell crabs, cleaned

2 teaspoons prepared horseradish

4 tablespoons balsamic vinegar

6 tablespoons unsalted butter

6 tablespoons all-purpose flour

8 cups mixed greens

Salt and freshly ground black pepper

6 tablespoons white wine

4 tablespoons cold butter

2 cups crumbled blue cheese

IN the evenings, especially in summer toward the end of crawfish season when the restaurant was slow, my dad used to take us out to the Chef Pass—a narrow, winding bit of water through which the saltwater of the Gulf flowed into Lake Pontchartrain by way of Lake Borgne. The pass was incredibly rich in nutrients, plus it had a very strong tidal surge that brought in shrimp like crazy. There was a serious fishing community at the Pass, with lots of buying and selling of fish, shrimp, and crabs. My dad would always mix business with pleasure, drinking a beer with the local guys to find out where the fish were biting and on what kind of bait. Then he'd find out who had what and go and buy that for the restaurant.

For me as a kid, this was great. We usually got to play some games, because each little restaurant or bar had a bowling machine or, my favorite, a mechanical bear you could shoot with a rifle and he'd roar. As that "something extra" the old Creoles called lagniappe, we got to be around these crabby old fishing kind of people. They were the mountain men of the marsh.

Our boat, a modified Lafitte skiff called *Miss Toto,* was docked at a place called Cochran Shipyards. I was always fascinated by that shipyard, not just for the crusty characters who hung around but also for the turn-of-the-century oyster boats being worked on there. I learned by asking questions: these were old sailing schooners that the local folks called Biloxi luggers. What impressed me most was the workmanship of their curved wooden sterns.

Since there wasn't all that long before dark by the time we'd get to the shipyard and we kids were always antsy to catch something, we'd climb into *Miss Toto* and my dad would steer straight for the croaker hole. I can't think of croakers—a poor relation of the same family that gives us redfish—without thinking of croaker holes. I know there's a lot of fish in the sea, but for me as a kid, going fishing meant going for croakers.

We'd end up at a marshy island that's no longer there because of all the storms. We'd anchor there, and, if we were lucky, the croakers would wait until we got our lines in before they started letting themselves be caught.

Few things in life come with any guarantees, but fishing for croakers in a croaker hole has got to be one of them. They put up a good fight, especially if you have two on different hooks on the same line and they are both pulling toward the bottom. There I'd be, reeling and grinning, stocking an ice chest or two in just a couple of hours. Of course, even our family couldn't put away all the croakers we piled into ice chests at Chef Pass. The next day my dad would feature two whole fried croakers with french fries at the restaurant— for 99 cents. I figured it was great business because we hadn't had to pay anybody for the fish. My dad always pointed out that, well, somebody had to pay for the gas!

There are plenty of good things you can do in the kitchen with croakers. For my money, it's hard to beat simply battering them whole with cornmeal and frying them. Whole croakers can be served traditionally with tartar or cocktail sauce, or upgraded a little with a garlic sauce like my mother used to make for shrimp, crab, crawfish, or even fried chicken.

The meat of a croaker is incredibly sweet. The bad news for some people is that there are a lot of tiny bones. I actually think croaker is one of the very best eating fish, if you have the patience and artistry to deal with the bones.

Redfish Court Bouillon

Serves 6

Redfish court bouillon is a traditional Creole fish stew in which everything is cooked together until it has a united flavor. Experimenting with the main elements in my kitchen, I've found that this classic recipe updates extremely well along the lines I suggest here.

CUT each fillet in half. On a large plate, dredge the redfish fillets in the seasoned flour and shake off any excess. Heat the olive oil and butter in a large frying pan over medium heat and briefly sauté the fish on both sides, 1 to 2 minutes on each side. Drain on paper towels and discard the excess oil.

In a bowl, combine the crushed and the diced tomatoes. Deglaze the pan with the white wine, scraping the browned bits from the bottom of the pan, and add the tomatoes, lemons, Italian seasoning, pepper, and fish stock. Cook 2 to 3 minutes. Transfer the fish to a heated plate. Add the salt to the broth and reduce by half over high heat, 3 to 4 minutes.

Remove the lemon slices. Place the rice on individual plates, place a fillet on the rice, top with the sauce, and serve immediately.

3 (8- to 10-ounce) redfish fillets, skin removed

1 cup seasoned flour (page 145)

2 tablespoons olive oil

2 tablespoons butter

2 (8-ounce) cans crushed tomatoes, with juice

1 cup diced fresh plum tomatoes

1/2 cup white wine

4 lemons, sliced crosswise

1 1/2 teaspoons Italian seasoning (page 149)

1 1/2 teaspoons coarsely ground black pepper

1 cup fish stock (page 148) or clam juice

1/2 teaspoon salt

3 cups steamed white rice

Pecan Trout with Honey Cream Sauce

Serves 4

Whitewash

1 egg

2 cups milk

¼ cup all-purpose flour

1 cup shelled pecans

½ cup all-purpose flour

4 (6- to 7-ounce) speckled trout fillets

¼ cup peanut oil

1 cup heavy whipping cream

2 tablespoons honey

Contrast is the key word with this lucky accident of a recipe, a notion that blends the crunch and flavor of pecans with the smooth sweetness of the honey and cream. Now that I've tasted this dish, the whole process seems magical. But all I was doing was working through in my head what Louisiana country people would have on hand for cooking some nice trout.

TO prepare the whitewash, in a medium bowl, use a whisk to beat together the egg, milk, and flour until incorporated and smooth.

Grind the pecans in a blender until they are the texture of fine sand and mix with the flour in a large bowl.

Dip each of the trout fillets in the whitewash and then coat on both sides with the pecan mixture. Sauté quickly in the peanut oil over medium heat, just until the fillets are flecked with golden brown on both sides, about 2 minutes per side.

To prepare the sauce, combine the cream and honey in a small saucepan over medium-high heat, simmering until it is reduced by about half, about 15 minutes. To serve, place 1 trout fillet on each plate and spoon the sauce over the top.

Blackened Tuna

Serves 4

If you think you know blackened redfish or blackened anything else—a technique that became both a blessing and a curse throughout the Cajun-crazed 1980s—you might think again, particularly if you hate burnt, dry fish as much as I do. The recipe we use at the restaurant preserves the spicy coating of the original, but it adds the butter after, not before, the fish is coated. I know it's an adjustment from the recipe used in so many real (and not-so-real) Cajun cookbooks, but the biggest adjustment is that this one tastes good!

PREHEAT the oven to 400 degrees.

Roll the fillets in the blackening seasoning, coating each generously, and dip in the melted butter. Heat a cast-iron skillet over high heat and carefully set the fish into it. Considerable smoke may result, but leave the fish in the skillet for 45 seconds per side—and no longer. Transfer the fillets to a baking pan and cook in the oven for 5 to 7 minutes for rare. Serve on dinner plates.

4 (6- to 7-ounce) skinless fresh tuna (or redfish or swordfish) fillets, 1/2 inch to 2/3 inch thick

1/4 cup blackening seasoning (page 145)

1/4 cup melted butter

Amberjack with Oysters and Artichoke Hearts

Serves 4

Sauce

4 red bell peppers

2 teaspoons Asian chile
    paste

2 teaspoons salt

6 tablespoons paprika

2 tablespoons finely
    ground black pepper

2 teaspoons coarsely
    ground black pepper

2 tablespoons ground
    white pepper

2 teaspoons ground red
    pepper

2 teaspoons dried thyme

4 teaspoons salt

4 (8-ounce) amberjack fil-
    lets, skinned

2 teaspoons plus 6 table-
    spoons butter, melted

2 cups white wine

$^2/_3$ cup rinsed and
    drained artichoke
    hearts, quartered

20 medium raw oysters
    (1 cup)

1 cup oyster water

2 cups (5 ounces) loosely
    packed fresh spinach

This has been a hit since day one. I created this for any fish that has a steaklike texture and that benefits from careful cooking. Of those fish served around New Orleans, amberjack is a solid choice. You can also use tuna or swordfish. As for the rest of the preparation, this city loves anything using oysters and artichokes.

TO make the sauce, roast the peppers evenly over an open flame until they are charred black and then place them directly in a bowl of ice water. Remove the charred skin. Place the peppers in a food processor fitted with the metal blade and purée. Stir in the chile paste and salt and set aside.

Preheat the oven to 350 degrees.

In a small bowl, combine all of the seasonings. Sprinkle the seasonings generously over the fillets, and then dip the coated fillets in the 6 tablespoons of melted butter. Sauté in a preheated skillet over medium-high heat, cooking until browned on both sides, 1 to 2 minutes. Transfer the fish to a baking sheet. Pour the butter from the skillet over the fillets and bake in the oven for 15 minutes.

Pour the wine into the skillet and deglaze, scraping up the browned bits from the pan, then reduce over high heat to $^1/_2$ cup. Remove from the heat and reserve.

In a separate skillet over medium heat, melt the remaining 2 teaspoons butter and add the artichoke hearts, sautéing just until heated through. Add the oysters and oyster water, stirring until the liquid evaporates. Add the wine reduction and spinach, tossing gently until the spinach is wilted and hot.

To serve, divide the vegetable mixture between 4 plates and top with the amberjack. Top each fillet with the bell pepper sauce. Serve immediately.

Trout Florentine

Serves 4

Trout may be the best fish to use in this variation on a European classic, but I've also enjoyed considerable success with redfish, drum, and sheepshead. Any thin-fillet, mild-tasting fish works well. If all you have available fresh is a thicker fish, just slice the fillets thin and they should work fine. One additional plus about this recipe is that you can finish the construction and just pop it in the oven when it's showtime.

PREHEAT the oven to 400 degrees.

In a shallow pan, season the water with the pepper, bay leaves, salt, and lemon. Heat this liquid to a simmer, add the fish fillets, and poach 1 minute per side. Remove the trout from the poaching liquid with a slotted spoon and set the trout aside.

To prepare the sauce, reduce the cream by half in a medium saucepan over high heat, about 3 minutes. Sauté the spinach in a small pan over medium heat with the butter, garlic, and pepper for 1 minute. Stir in the reduced cream and 1 cup of the cheese.

Immediately pour the sauce into a baking dish and gently place the poached fish fillets on the sauce. Sprinkle with the remaining cheese, season with the Italian seasoning, and lightly cover with a layer of the bread crumbs. Bake in the oven for 8 to 10 minutes. Remove from the oven and serve immediately.

4 cups water

2 tablespoons coarsely ground black pepper

4 bay leaves

2 teaspoons salt

1 lemon

4 (6- to 8-ounce) speckled trout fillets

Sauce

2 cups heavy whipping cream

4 cups (10 ounces) loosely packed fresh spinach

2 tablespoons butter

2 teaspoons minced garlic

1 teaspoon coarsely ground black pepper

1½ cups freshly grated white Cheddar cheese

2 tablespoons Italian seasoning (page 149)

½ cup Italian-style bread crumbs

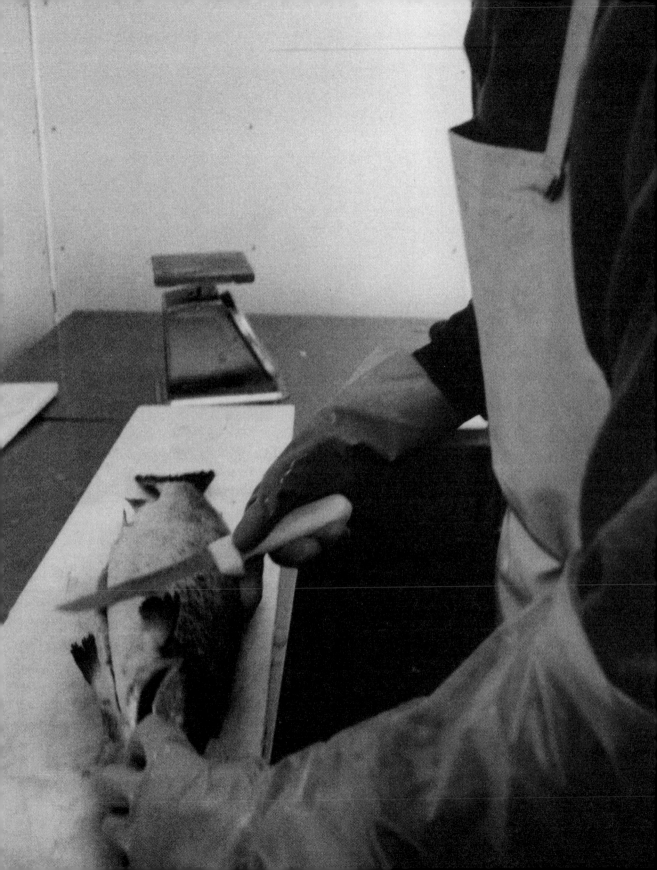

8 TRICKS FOR PERFECT FRYING

1. The food you're going to fry should always be good.

2. The whitewash should always be cold.

3. The oils should always be hot, about 350 degrees. If a drop of batter sizzles in the oil, it's probably hot enough.

4. Do not overcrowd your fry batches, and give your oil time to recover after each batch (returning to 350 degrees).

5. Skim excess particles from the fry oil with a fine wire skimmer after each batch.

6. The coating should stay as dry as possible. If it becomes too wet, replace it with more dry coating.

7. Always use enough oil to submerge the food.

8. Make sure to drain excess oil by placing the fried foods on paper towels.

Asparagus-Lemon-Cream Trout

Serves 4

4 (6- to 8-ounce) speckled trout fillets

Salt

Freshly ground black pepper

24 spears fresh asparagus, trimmed and blanched

2 cups heavy whipping cream

1 teaspoon grated lemon zest

1 teaspoon coarsely ground black pepper

1/4 teaspoon salt

Sometimes you try a combination and just get lucky. That was the case with this unusual technique, which involves rolling fresh asparagus in trout fillets and poaching them. The lemon-cream sauce seemed to work better than anything, bringing the simple, fresh tastes already in the main ingredients right up in front.

SEASON the trout to taste with salt and pepper. Set 6 spears of the asparagus crosswise across each fillet and roll the fish pinwheel style around the spears. Wrap each roll tightly in plastic wrap, fold ends to make a complete seal, and place in a shallow pan with rapidly boiling water for 5 to 7 minutes to poach.

To prepare the sauce, combine all of the remaining ingredients in a pan and reduce by about half over medium-high heat, 3 to 4 minutes.

To serve, remove the fish fillets from the water and peel off and discard the plastic wrap. Set 1 roll on each plate and divide the sauce evenly over the top of the fish.

Fried Catfish

Serves 6

Whitewash

1 egg

2 cups milk

1/4 cup all-purpose flour

3 pounds fresh catfish fillets

1 pound cornmeal

Vegetable oil for deep-frying

Cocktail sauce (page 146)

As a kid, I ate catfish whose pedigree and dietary habits I didn't want to know. These were the channel cats and gafftops that stole your bait all day until they took your hook by accident or had the bad luck of swimming into your shrimp net. Those days are pretty much forgotten now, considering the high quality of farm-raised catfish. For sheer easy eating, it's hard to beat these fried catfish strips.

PREPARE the whitewash by combining the egg, milk, and flour in a bowl, whisking until smooth. Cut the catfish fillets in diagonal strips and dip each strip into the whitewash. Dredge the catfish in the cornmeal, shake off the excess, and fry in a deep-fryer in vegetable oil preheated to 350 degrees until golden brown and crispy. Serve immediately with cocktail sauce.

Sicilian Baked Fish

Serves 4

No, this isn't one of my mother's recipes, but it could be. Baked fish is very popular at my restaurant, and I love the ingredients for Sicilian preparations, so I thought about what ingredients would come together tasting like Sicily on a piece of fish. Here is the result.

PREHEAT the oven to 350 degrees.

To prepare the pesto sauce, combine the basil, garlic, pine nuts, olive oil, salt, and cheese in a medium bowl.

Heat the olive oil in a medium saucepan over medium heat; add the tomatoes, artichoke hearts, olives, capers, and crushed pepper; and sauté for 5 minutes. Add the spinach and stir just until it wilts. Remove the pan from the heat.

Coat each fish fillet with the pesto sauce and place in a baking pan. Sprinkle with a little water to keep moist. Cover the pan tightly with aluminum foil and bake for 5 to 10 minutes, depending on the thickness of the fish.

To serve, place 1 piece of fish on each plate and top with some of the sautéed vegetable mixture.

Pesto Sauce

1/2 cup tightly packed fresh basil

1/2 cup chopped garlic (6 large cloves)

1/4 cup pine nuts

1/2 cup virgin olive oil

1/2 teaspoon salt

2 tablespoons freshly grated Parmesan cheese

2 tablespoons olive oil

1 cup chopped plum tomatoes

1/2 cup quartered artichoke hearts, rinsed and drained

1/3 cup kalamata olives, rinsed and drained

1 tablespoon capers, rinsed and drained

1 teaspoon crushed red pepper

1 cup fresh spinach

4 (6- to 8-ounce) fresh amberjack, snapper, or puppy drum fillets

Chilled Tuna Remoulade

Remoulade Sauce

2 anchovy fillets

½ tablespoon freshly
   squeezed lime juice

½ cup mayonnaise

½ cup Creole mustard

1 teaspoon white wine

⅛ teaspoon Tabasco
   sauce

½ teaspoon paprika

Poaching Liquid

1 cup white wine

2 tablespoons fresh dill

1 lemon, sliced and
   squeezed, with rind
   reserved

1 teaspoon coarsely
   ground black pepper

1 tablespoon chopped
   garlic

1 bay leaf

4 (4- to 6-ounce) tuna
   steaks

½ cup chopped fresh
   tomatoes

1 tablespoon cold butter

Fresh dill sprigs, for
   garnish

Serves 4

I think shrimp remoulade is one of the greatest creations of the Creole mind, but that doesn't stop me during the long, hot summer months from putting the pungent sauce that is its signature to other interesting uses. Since just about everybody loves fresh tuna—and since it has been a new catch in the Gulf these past few years—here's what I do to pull a quick one on the usual shrimp. You'll like the warm sauce beneath the chilled tuna and remoulade.

TO prepare the remoulade sauce, mash the anchovy fillets with the lime juice in a bowl until a paste is formed, and stir in the remaining ingredients. Cover the bowl with plastic wrap and place in the refrigerator to chill for at least 3 hours.

To prepare the poaching liquid, mix together all of the ingredients for the liquid in a medium pan and simmer over medium heat. Add the tuna and poach for 2 to 3 minutes. Remove the tuna from the pan, reserving the poaching liquid. Cover the tuna with plastic wrap and chill on a plate in the refrigerator for about 1 hour.

Add the tomatoes to the reserved poaching liquid. Boil over high heat until reduced by half, 3 to 4 minutes, and then strain. Whisk in the butter to finish the sauce. Keep warm.

To serve, spoon 2 tablespoons of the warm sauce into each of 4 small bowls. Place 1 piece of the chilled tuna in each bowl and top with 2 teaspoons of the refrigerated remoulade sauce. Garnish with fresh dill and serve.

Fried Fresh Whole Croaker

Serves 4

Here's the classic way to cook croaker when you bring it home fresh from the croaker hole. Any number of sauces can be served on the side, or you can enjoy the sweet meat of the fish all by itself.

TO prepare the whitewash, in a medium bowl, use a whisk to beat together the egg, milk, and flour until incorporated and smooth.

Heat the oil in a heavy skillet over medium heat. Cut 3 diagonal slices in the side of each fish. In a separate bowl, mix together the ingredients for the seasoned cornmeal. Spread the cornmeal out onto a plate. Coat the fish on all sides in the whitewash and then coat it completely in the cornmeal mixture. Fry the fish in the oil until it floats. Squeeze the lemon juice on the fish and serve hot.

Whitewash
2 cups milk
1 egg
1/4 cup all-purpose flour

Vegetable oil for deep-frying
4 fresh croakers or other Gulf fish, head on, gutted and scaled, 1 to 1 1/4 pounds each

Seasoned Cornmeal
1 cup cornmeal
2 teaspoons salt
1 teaspoon freshly ground red pepper
2 teaspoons freshly ground black pepper
2 teaspoons garlic powder

Juice of 3 to 4 lemons

Croaker Meunière with Roasted Pecans

Serves 4

1/4 cup plus 1 tablespoon unsalted butter

4 (6- to 8-ounce) fresh croaker fillets or other 6-ounce fish fillets

2 cups seasoned flour (page 145)

1 cup white wine

1/2 teaspoon grated lemon zest

1/2 teaspoon Worcestershire sauce

1/2 cup roasted pecans

This variation on the famous trout dish solves the problem of the pin-bones—by removing them. However, be careful as you're boning this fish; it's harder than most to turn into a safely boneless delicacy. The rest is easy.

PREHEAT the oven to 350 degrees.

Dredge the fish fillets in the seasoned flour, shaking off any excess. In a sauté pan, melt 1/4 cup of the butter over medium heat. Brown the fish fillets on both sides, 1 minute per side, and transfer the fish to a baking pan, reserving the butter in the pan. Cook the fish in the oven for 3 to 4 minutes.

To prepare the sauce, discard all but 1/4 cup of the browned butter. Deglaze the pan with the white wine, scraping up the browned bits from the pan, and add the lemon zest and Worcestershire sauce. Reduce over high heat by half, about 3 minutes. Add the pecans and stir in the remaining 1 tablespoon butter.

To serve, place a piece of fish on each plate and top with some of the sauce. Serve hot.

Amberjack Sandwich

Serves 4

Everybody around New Orleans makes a pretty decent fried fish po-boy. But I found myself wanting something more: a different-tasting fish on a different type of bread. The result was this Mediterranean beauty, which gets a final burst of flavor from balsamic vinegar. You can use any firm-fleshed fish in this sandwich.

TO prepare the red bell peppers, roast the peppers over a flame, submerge in a bowl of cold water, and peel off all charred bits of skin. Remove the seeds, cut in julienne, and set aside.

Preheat the oven to 350 degrees.

To prepare the sauce, combine the relish with the balsamic vinegar in a small pan. Reduce the liquid by half over medium-high heat, 2 to 3 minutes, and set aside.

Dredge the amberjack in the seasoned flour, shaking off any excess. Sauté the fish in a skillet over medium heat in half the olive oil, about 1 minute per side, then transfer to a baking pan and finish cooking in the oven, about 5 minutes.

Brush the bread with a little of the remaining olive oil and toast in the preheated oven on a baking rack until crisp.

Sauté the tomatoes, spinach, and squash in the remaining oil in a medium pan over medium-high heat until the spinach is wilted, 4 to 5 minutes. Add 4 tablespoons of the reduced balsamic vinegar sauce.

To assemble, layer the bread, sautéed vegetables, roasted peppers, and fish 3 times, ending with the fish. Top each open-face sandwich with about 2 tablespoons of the sauce.

---

2 red bell peppers

4 tablespoons dill pickle relish

$1/2$ cup balsamic vinegar

12 (4-ounce) pieces of amberjack, cut $1/4$ inch thick

2 cups seasoned flour (page 145)

$1/2$ cup olive oil

12 thin slices baguette

2 large plum tomatoes, seeded and cut into 8 slices each

2 loosely packed cups fresh spinach, washed and stemmed

2 summer squash, seeded and julienned

CRAWFISH hail from a rich, watery area to the west of New Orleans known as the Atchafalaya Basin. The Atchafalaya is a river, a big river, with wild bursts of current in places. But New Orleans is most interested in its crawfish. There's an unofficial "crawfish zone" stretching from Pierre Part to Breaux Bridge, accurately billing itself as "The Crawfish Capital of the World."

I can tell you firsthand about the basin. It may not be a jungle out there, but it sure is one serious swamp. When I was eight or nine years old, I'm sure with my dad's sadistic encouragement, a friend of his named Charlie Rappo invited me to go crawfishing. He was an adult, and so was his son, who joined us, which meant that the same green water that came to their waists reached right up under my chin. Maybe you can picture me going from crawfish trap to crawfish trap through this awful muck, with ratty-looking nutria swimming around, cottonmouth moccasins slithering through the thick algae, probably an old gator or two hidden by the hanging moss. I was terrified, and I must have looked it.

We caught about fifty pounds of crawfish that day, those many years ago, enough to have a decent-sized family crawfish boil with some left over for a pot of étouffée. But as far as I was concerned, there had to be 8,000 better ways to get my hands on crawfish. I think that day was enough swamp to last me a lifetime.

Traveling the basin with my father, I also caught a glimpse of another way of catching crawfish, one that, happily, didn't involve swamp water under your chin. A lot of oldtimers fished along the banks with a special kind of net that hung by twine from a cane pole. Essentially, this net sat on the bottom with fish or chicken chunks for bait tied in the middle. Crawfish would saunter on over for the bait, then get caught when the oldtimer lifted the net out of the water. This method made a lot more sense to me.

But none of this crawfishing for dinner or crawfishing for fun figured into my life. In my family, crawfish were big, big business, even when they were bringing just four cents a pound. In his best seasons, my dad sold more than a million pounds of crawfish, most of which were delivered to us by three or four trucks a day coming in from the basin. The profit margin was tiny and the competition cut-throat, with customers driving across town because somebody had crawfish a penny cheaper. My dad didn't lose many battles in this war, I'll tell you that much.

The real deal for us was not fishing for crawfish but fishing for people who would sell us crawfish, good times and bad. I can't count how many road trips my father made, stopping for a beer or two at every bend in every mud or shell road in the Atchafalaya Basin. This was partly about family, since my father's mother came from just outside St. Martinville on Bayou Teche; but it was also about friendship and trust among near-strangers who needed each other. My dad needed crawfish, obviously. But the people with crawfish needed somebody who would take their product every time, pay as agreed in cash, and just generally be there for them, as my father was already there for so many in the city. This way, supply of and demand for crawfish could dance all over the map, without anybody (quite literally) getting left holding the bag.

The arrival of a truck bearing sacks of crawfish was, for us Jaegers, the beginning more than the end of a process. First, these mud dwellers had to be separated from all the unpleasantness that showed up with them: dirt, weeds, pieces of fish, and plenty of dead brothers and sisters. Crawfish are only good when they go into the boiling pot alive, though some other boilers didn't care as much about this as my dad did. His crawfish had to be perfect. So, we built a slanting chute that reminded me of chutes used in the California gold rush. Crawfish were my family's gold, in a way. A door let a few crawfish at a time move turtle-slow down the ramp; we'd clean them off really well before they reached the hamper. If a crawfish didn't move, it was dead and had to be tossed aside. Some were so slow, though, that picking out dead ones seemed like a flip of the coin.

We boiled ton after ton of crawfish in big stainless steel vats my father found somewhere. In his hands, the vats became boilers, with propane connected to produce the flame that heated the water that filled the air with fragrant spices. I stood there, stirring the crawfish in this huge vat with a paddle, my whole body dripping with sweat. If you can't stand the heat, you'd better not be born a Jaeger.

As a kid, I loved those vats because of what happened at the end of crawfish season. When the boiling was through, my dad let us fill the vats with cool, clear water. We had four or five vats, which meant that four or five of us kids had our own personal little swimming pool. I'm just glad nobody turned on the gas and tried to cook us!

One last crawfish story that must be told is about my father, his Cadillac, and the first batch of the season. Dad absolutely had to have the first crawfish in New Orleans. Since this was before the trucks started making their runs, my father took his brand new Cadillac into the Atchafalaya Basin and loaded the whole back seat with sacks of live crawfish. His friends were horrified.

"Charlie!" they shouted, so upset they couldn't form sentences —which means they were *really* upset (though a lot of them couldn't form sentences anyway!). "How could you? Once that crawfish smell gets in your car, it'll never come out."

My father stayed calm. "Listen," I heard him explain again and again. "Those crawfish paid for this Cadillac!"

Crawfish Étouffée

Serves 6

1/2 cup margarine

1 cup all-purpose flour

1/4 cup butter

1 cup chopped onions

1 cup chopped celery

1 cup chopped green bell
peppers

1 pound crawfish tail
meat, peeled

2 bay leaves

1 tablespoon grated
lemon zest

1/4 cup sherry

1/2 tablespoon freshly
ground black pepper

1/2 tablespoon blackening
seasoning (page 145)

3 tablespoons Crystal hot
sauce or other
Louisiana hot sauce

1/2 tablespoon Tabasco
sauce

1/2 tablespoon freshly
ground red pepper

1/2 tablespoon chile
powder

1 tablespoon salt

3 cups chicken stock

4 cups steamed white
rice

Here's a classic Cajun dish that's also a bit Deep South. Étouffée, after all, is French for "smothered," a reference to the habit of some cooks to cover the pot during cooking. I leave the pot uncovered, but that doesn't mean this dish lacks flavor. It takes a deep, almost nutty taste from the dark-brown roux. And if you think it tastes great the day you make it, give it a try the next day; like a lot of New Orleans food, it tastes even better!

T O prepare a roux, heat the margarine in a heavy skillet over medium heat and whisk in the flour. Cook, stirring constantly, until dark brown, 8 to 10 minutes. The roux should be the color of coffee grounds. Remove from the heat but continue to stir. Set aside.

Melt the butter in a large pot and sauté the onions, celery, and green peppers over medium heat until the onions are translucent, about 3 minutes. Add all of the remaining ingredients and stir in the roux. Cook the étouffée over medium heat until thick and bubbly, about 20 minutes.

Serve warm on individual plates over steamed rice.

TIPS FOR MAKING ROUX

Making a roux is a real art form, so here are some tips.

It is always best to use a heavy iron skillet, but a sauté pan will do. You may use any type of oil, butter, or margarine, but I don't recommend olive oil.

First, heat the oil to the smoking point. Add half the flour and start whisking. Keep whisking the roux as long as it is warm. Once the flour and oil start to brown, whisk in more flour until the flour is incorporated. The object is to brown, not burn, the mixture; the roux will not burn as long as you keep whisking it. Depending on the heat you use, this could take 5 to 20 minutes to finish. Be patient! The longer you cook, the darker the color. In Cajun cooking the preferred color is that of coffee grounds, but a peanut butter color will do.

When you are close to reaching the final stage, turn off the heat and continue whisking the mixture until it has cooked somewhat. If you don't keep whisking, it will burn at this stage. Do not let the hot roux touch your skin. It will burn you unless it has cooled completely.

Roux will last for months if stored in an airtight container in the refrigerator. Adding roux to thicken and flavor any soup or stew will instantly Cajunize it.

Crawfish Corn Chowder

Serves 6 to 8

2 cups chopped celery

2 cups chopped onions

1/2 cup butter

4 cups corn kernels

3 cups peeled and diced potatoes

1 pound crawfish tails, with fat

1/4 cup chopped fresh parsley

2 cups chicken stock (page 149)

2 quarts milk

1 cup heavy whipping cream

1/4 cup sherry

Salt and freshly ground white pepper

Whitewash

1 egg

2 cups water

1/4 cup all-purpose flour

I see this lush yet delicate chowder as a combination of two important southern Louisiana traditions: the cream-based soup recalls the French, and the corn is an ingredient the Cajuns picked up from local Indians.

IN a medium pot, sauté the celery and onions in the butter over medium heat until the onions are translucent. Add the corn, potatoes, crawfish, parsley, and chicken stock; increase the heat; and boil until the potatoes are tender, about 10 minutes. Add the milk, cream, and sherry and season to taste with salt and white pepper.

To prepare the whitewash, in a medium bowl, use a whisk to beat together the egg, water, and flour until incorporated and smooth. Blend the whitewash into the other chowder ingredients and cook over medium heat until thickened and no flour taste remains, about 10 minutes. Serve in deep bowls.

Crawfish, Chicken, and Andouille Gumbo

Serves 10

This local classic, made with chicken and our andouille sausage, is often called Gumbo Ya-Ya—a colorful African-sounding name if there ever was one. Still, during crawfish season, we like to take the recipe one better. I don't know, maybe this version should be called Gumbo Yeah-Yeah. At least that's what you'll say about it when you taste a spoonful.

BROWN the andouille sausage in a large soup pot over medium heat, 3 to 4 minutes, and remove the sausage from the pan. Set the pan and the sausage aside. In a separate skillet, melt 2 cups of the margarine and stir in the flour. Cook, stirring constantly, over medium heat to produce a smooth, medium-brown roux (see page 105 for tips on making the roux). Remove the pan from the heat. Add some of the diced onions and celery and set aside.

Add the remaining 3 tablespoons margarine and the onions and celery to the soup pot, stirring to scrape up brown bits of the sausage from the bottom of the pan. Cook until the onions are translucent, 5 to 6 minutes. Add all of the remaining ingredients except for the filé powder and rice. Add the roux a little at a time, stirring until the gumbo is thick enough to hold up the vegetables and the liquid is heated to a slow boil. Stir in the reserved andouille and cook over medium heat for 45 minutes, until the flavors marry and the roux is thoroughly incorporated.

Serve in bowls over steamed rice. Sprinkle each bowl with filé powder.

NOTE: We like to make big pots of food in New Orleans. This is how we make new friends—feed a hungry family and keep in touch with their neighbors. So bring a couple of containers to work the next day and give them away. I promise you will loosen up the tightest co-worker. You might even get a raise!

2 pounds andouille sausage

2 cups plus 3 tablespoons margarine

2 cups all-purpose flour

4 cups diced onions

4 cups diced celery

2 cups dry sherry

4 large bay leaves

2 pounds crawfish meat, peeled

2 pounds chicken, diced

2 tablespoons liquid hickory smoke (optional)

4 tablespoons Crystal hot sauce or other Louisiana hot sauce

1 tablespoon Tabasco sauce

1 tablespoon freshly ground black pepper

5 tablespoons Worcestershire sauce

1 tablespoon freshly ground red pepper

2 gallons chicken stock (page 149)

2 tablespoons salt

4 tablespoons filé powder

5 cups steamed white rice

Crawfish Cakes

Serves 6

Everybody fixes crab cakes these days, so we went the extra mile for a crawfish variation. It sells like, well, crab cakes! Anyway, the recipe produces a wonderful crawfish stuffing you can use any way you want—as cakes for sautéing, as round Cajun "boulettes" for deep-frying, or as stuffing for fish or even double-cut pork chops, a favorite of mine.

MELT the ½ cup butter in a medium pot and add the onions, celery, green peppers, and garlic. Sauté over medium heat until the onions are translucent, about 3 minutes. Add the remaining ingredients except for bread, bread crumbs, and seasoned flour and stir to thoroughly combine. Remove from the heat and set the mixture aside.

Soak the bread in water for 1 minute and squeeze out the excess by pressing the bread in a colander with your hands. Stir the bread into the crawfish-vegetable mixture and fold in the bread crumbs. Cook over medium heat for 5 to 7 minutes. Remove from the heat and let cool. Roll the mixture into ½-cup balls and gently press them down with the palm of your hand to form 3-inch cakes. Dust with the seasoned flour. Sauté in a sauté pan with the remaining butter over medium heat until golden brown, about 1 minute on each side. Cook no more than 5 at a time. Drain on paper towels and serve warm.

NOTES: A boulette is a stuffing that is rolled into a small ball and deep-fried. Take some of this stuffing, roll it in seasoned flour (page 145), and deep-fry it to golden-brown. Place 2 or 3 on top of your etouffée for a flavorful garnish. They also make a great party appetizer served with cocktail sauce (page 146).

You can also take that stuffing and fill a double-cut pork chop that has been sliced down the middle. Season the pork chops with blackening seasoning (page 145) and bake until done.

You can also replace the crab in creamy crab sauce (page 147) with equal amounts of crawfish meat and pour it over your crawfish cakes or pork chop.

Ingredients

- ½ cup plus 2 to 3 tablespoons butter
- ¾ cup chopped onions
- ¾ cup chopped celery
- ¾ cup chopped green peppers
- 2 cloves garlic, chopped
- 3 tablespoons Crystal hot sauce or other Louisiana hot sauce
- 3 tablespoons Worcestershire sauce
- 3 tablespoons Creole mustard
- 1 tablespoon salt
- 1½ teaspoons freshly ground black pepper
- 1½ teaspoons Tabasco sauce
- 1½ teaspoons freshly squeezed lemon juice
- ½ pound finely chopped crawfish meat
- ½ pound whole crawfish tail meat
- ½ loaf day-old French bread
- 1½ cups Italian-style bread crumbs
- 1 cup seasoned flour (page 145)

Fried Eggplant Medallions with Crawfish Sauce

Serves 6 to 8

The Sicilians and the Creoles have been interacting in the New Orleans kitchen so long it's hard to tell who showed up with what. Simply put, anything using eggplant around here is Sicilian, since they learned about it many centuries ago from the Greeks, who learned about it from the Turks. While I'm a great fan of this spicy crawfish sauce, I admit to eating the fried eggplant all by itself, sprinkled with a little pecorino-romano cheese.

PLACE the eggplant in 2 cups of salted water for 30 minutes to reduce the acidity. Drain and pat dry with paper towels.

To prepare the sauce, melt the butter in a large pan over medium heat and sauté the andouille and tasso until almost crispy, 3 to 5 minutes. Add the chicken stock and the chopped and crushed tomatoes and cook over medium heat until the liquid is reduced by half, about 5 minutes. Add the crawfish, sherry, and green onions and reduce by half again, about 4 minutes. Keep the sauce warm over low heat.

In a medium bowl, use a whisk to beat together the whitewash ingredients. To prepare the eggplant, drain the rounds, dredge them in the flour, dip them in the whitewash, and coat them with the bread crumbs. Fry the medallions in the oil until golden brown on each side, about 3 minutes.

To serve, transfer the fried eggplant medallions to individual plates and top with the crawfish sauce.

1 eggplant, sliced crosswise in 1/2-inch-thick rounds

1 tablespoon butter

3 ounces andouille sausage, sliced

1/4 cup tasso, diced

1/2 cup chicken stock (page 149)

1/2 cup chopped fresh tomatoes

1 (8-ounce) can crushed whole tomatoes

1/2 pound crawfish tail meat, peeled

1/4 cup sherry

1/2 cup finely chopped green onions

1 cup seasoned flour (page 145)

Whitewash

1 egg

2 cups water

1/4 cup all-purpose flour

1 cup Italian-style bread crumbs

1 cup vegetable oil for frying

Popcorn Crawfish

Serves 6

Whitewash

1 egg

2 cups water

¼ cup all-purpose flour

½ cup all-purpose flour

½ teaspoon chile powder

½ teaspoon ground red
pepper

½ teaspoon finely
ground black pepper

½ teaspoon salt

1 pound crawfish tails,
peeled

1 cup Italian-style bread
crumbs

Vegetable oil for deep-
frying

This dish has become a hit in recent years because it's so easy and the crunchy mouthfuls are fun to munch. I'd rather watch a movie popping these babies into my mouth any time.

IN a medium bowl, use a whisk to beat together the whitewash ingredients.

Put the flour in a large bowl and season with the chile powder, peppers, and salt. Dredge the crawfish tails in the flour, then dip them in the whitewash, and quickly dredge them in the bread crumbs.

Deep-fry in oil heated to 350 degrees until golden brown, 2 to 3 minutes. Drain on paper towels and serve with cocktail sauce.

NOTE: These make a great appetizer served with cocktail sauce (page 146), in a po-boy sandwich (page 41; replace the shrimp with crawfish), or as a garnish for Crawfish Etouffée (page 104), Crawfish Chili (page 114), or Crawfish Picante (page 117).

How to Eat a Crawfish

Much lore and more than a few T-shirts sold in shops along Bourbon Street devote themselves to the art and science of eating crawfish. On one level, crawfish eating is a simple act of peeling the crustaceans. On the next level, it's a beer-blessed religious service ending with the—yes, you heard me—sucking of the heads. Yes, you heard me. But don't give up yet.

Though the crawfish is small (a true crawfish lover can down ten pounds of crawfish, which yields only one or two pounds of meat), it offers at least two distinct taste and texture sensations. One is the renowned sucking of the heads, in truth a kind of skilled slurping of the fat and spices that have accumulated in the top end of the shell. While viewed by some as a red badge of courage, it's all a matter of taste. We won't make fun of you if you don't do this.

Subtle, sweet crawfish tailmeat—the business end of the creature—is now sold prepeeled and frozen in its delicious orange fat in markets around the world. The fat is important for flavor in finished dishes, so don't wash it off. Trust me.

Eating a crawfish may take some practice, so there's no time like now to begin. Start by snapping the head and the tail of the cooked crawfish apart. If you're not a fan of the head, toss it aside and peel the tail. This can be done by cracking the hard shell down the side with your thumbs. Lift out the meat, remove the dark vein with a paring knife, and either devour the meat on the spot or toss it into a bowl for use in a recipe. If you're peeling crawfish for a dish, by the way, you're advised to cook extra to allow for all the tails you and other pickers won't be able to help eating.

As tasty as the tailmeat is, other parts of the crawfish make for good eating, too. Cajuns and Creoles can resemble a barbarian army that leaves nothing in its path when they get some crawfish into their hands. The tiny claws can be cracked open, picked, and sucked clean. The cavity of the bottom shell can even be explored, turning up a flavorful piece of yellow liver and more of that lush, silky crawfish fat. It all depends on how well you want to get to know your crawfish!

Crawfish Bread

Serves 8

Bread

¼ cup light brown sugar, firmly packed

1 tablespoon active dry yeast

1 cup warm water

5 to 6 cups all-purpose flour

1½ teaspoons salt

2 tablespoons chile powder

3 tablespoons extra virgin olive oil

Filling

2 tablespoons olive oil

2 tablespoons butter

½ cup chopped onions

2 cloves garlic, chopped

1 pound crawfish tails, peeled

2 tablespoons blackening seasoning (page 145)

Nobody I knew as a kid made anything like this crawfish bread, but a version of it has become one of the big hits of the annual New Orleans Jazz and Heritage Festival. This can be a main dish or just an incredible snack.

TO prepare the bread, in a large bowl mix the sugar and yeast in the warm water until dissolved. Allow to foam for 10 minutes. Add the flour, salt, and chile powder and mix until the dough just starts to come together. Add the olive oil 1 tablespoon at a time. The dough should be elastic, soft, and just slightly sticky. Form into a ball and place in a bowl coated with olive oil. Turn the dough to coat in the oil and cover loosely with a moist kitchen towel. Set the bowl in a warm place to rise until doubled in bulk, 60 to 90 minutes.

To prepare the filling, heat the olive oil and butter in a large pan over medium-high heat. Add the onions and sauté until they are translucent, 5 to 6 minutes. Add the rest of the filling ingredients and sauté for about 3 minutes. Remove the pan from the heat and allow to cool.

Punch the dough down and allow it to rise again, covered, for 20 to 25 minutes. Cut the dough in half and place the halves on a work surface. Roll out each half into a rectangle. Spread half of the crawfish mixture on each rectangle, leaving a 1-inch border at the edges. Roll the dough jelly roll style and pinch the seams together.

Preheat the oven to 350 degrees.

Cover with a cloth and allow to rise for 30 minutes, until it is puffy. Bake on a baking sheet lined with parchment paper on the center rack of the oven until golden brown, about 15 minutes. Remove from the oven and let stand 10 to 15 minutes before slicing. Serve sliced.

Crawfish-Tasso Mirlitons

Serves 6

In New Orleans, most people have never bought a mirliton. Some aunt or cousin always had a tree in the yard, and that meant everybody in the family ended up with a bag of mirlitons just waiting to be stuffed. Here's my favorite recipe for doing exactly that.

TO prepare the mirlitons, boil them in a pot of salted water until tender, about 20 minutes. Remove the mirlitons from the pot and, using a spoon, scoop out the meat to create a shell. Set the shells aside. Discard the seeds and chop the mirliton meat.

To prepare the stuffing, in a sauté pan over medium heat, sauté the chopped mirliton with the butter, onions, celery, and bell peppers for about 5 minutes, until the onions are translucent. Add the tasso, bay leaves, and crawfish tails, stirring to combine. Cook for 3 more minutes.

Soak the bread in water and drain the water by pressing the bread into a colander with your hands. Add the drained bread to the crawfish mixture and cook for 3 more minutes, stirring every 30 seconds or so. Add the chicken stock and reduce over medium-high heat until almost all of the liquid has evaporated, about 5 minutes. Add the remaining ingredients and stir to combine.

Preheat the oven to 350 degrees.

Stuff the crawfish mixture into the mirliton shells and bake uncovered on a baking sheet until browned, 8 to 10 minutes. Serve on individual plates.

3 mirlitons, halved lengthwise

2 tablespoons butter

1/2 cup chopped onions

1/2 cup chopped celery

1/2 cup chopped green bell peppers

1 cup finely chopped tasso

2 bay leaves

1 cup crawfish tails, peeled

1 1/2 cups cubed stale French bread

1 1/2 cups chicken stock (page 149)

1/4 cup chopped green onions

1/4 cup chopped fresh parsley

2 teaspoons Worcestershire sauce

4 teaspoons Crystal hot sauce or other Louisiana hot sauce

1 teaspoon Italian seasoning (page 149)

2 teaspoons coarsely ground black pepper

1/2 teaspoon salt

1/2 cup Italian-style bread crumbs

Crawfish Chili

Serves 8

1 cup diced onions

1 cup diced green bell peppers

2 pounds ground beef

2 pounds crawfish tail meat, peeled

2 (16-ounce) cans whole tomatoes, crushed

2 cups tomato sauce

4 tablespoons chile powder

4 tablespoons ground cumin

4 tablespoons garlic powder

1 teaspoon cayenne pepper

Toppings

Grated sharp Cheddar cheese

Chopped white onions

Fresh jalapeño peppers, sliced

Sour cream

I love the taste of good chili, so you can bet I'd end up playing around with crawfish in the mix. You can use just crawfish, of course, but I like what happens when you add a bit of ground beef, too. I love to eat a big old bowl of this on those rare icy days in New Orleans, or spoon it over chips and grate some cheese over the top to make killer nachos. If this is culinary slumming, then I never want to live too far from the slums.

IN a large pan, sauté the onions, green peppers, and ground beef over medium heat until the onions are translucent, about 5 minutes. Drain off the fat. Add the remaining ingredients except the toppings and cook until reduced and rich and thick, 30 to 40 minutes.

To serve, put the chili in bowls and sprinkle it with grated sharp Cheddar, chopped white onions, and sliced jalapeños. You could also add a dollop of sour cream. Or, pour the mixture over nachos or even a roasted chicken breast.

Crawfish Ravioli

Serves 6

If I told you every step it takes to make your own fresh pasta sheets, this recipe would take a lot longer to make. But, with the good frozen sheets available, I see no reason to devote lots of time to this project. To me, the excitement is in the garlicky, buttery crawfish filling and the silky brandy cream sauce. Invest your troops in the battles that matter, I like to say.

TO prepare the ravioli filling, in a bowl, combine the crawfish with the green onions and black pepper, and blend in the garlic butter until all of the ingredients are incorporated into a paste.

Place the pasta sheets on a work surface and place 1 tablespoon of the filling materials every 2$^1/_2$ inches. Cover with a second pasta sheet. With a sharp knife, cut the pasta into individual squares or triangles around the mounds of filling and seal the edges of the ravioli with the wet tines of a fork.

Drop the ravioli in a medium saucepan with boiling salted water, being careful not to overcrowd them. Cook the ravioli until they float, and then remove them from the water with a slotted spoon. Drain the ravioli in a colander and quickly transfer to serving plates. Divide the hot brandy cream sauce evenly among the servings, topping the ravioli with the sauce, and serve immediately.

NOTE: You can substitute regular butter for the garlic butter if you add 1 teaspoon of garlic powder or 1 tablespoon chopped garlic.

---

1 pound chopped crawfish

3 tablespoons finely sliced green onions

1 tablespoon coarsely ground black pepper

3 tablespoons garlic butter (page 146; see note)

4 prepared pasta sheets

1 cup hot brandy cream sauce (page 147)

Crawfish-Stuffed Peppers

Serves 6

¹/₂ cup butter

¹/₂ cup chopped onions

¹/₂ cup chopped celery

¹/₂ cup chopped green
bell peppers

¹/₂ pound ground chicken
livers

1 pound crawfish tails,
peeled

2 teaspoons blackening
seasoning (page 145)

1 teaspoon freshly
ground black pepper

2 teaspoons Tabasco
sauce

4 bay leaves

4 cups chicken stock
(page 149)

2 cups uncooked white
rice

¹/₄ cup finely chopped
green onions

Salt

6 green bell peppers,
tops sliced off, seed-
ed, and parboiled for
2 minutes

Here's a really old-timey New Orleans dish that's come back with the vengeance of, say, meatloaf and mashed potatoes in those chic, over-priced "diners" in New York and Los Angeles. Around my house growing up, anything that didn't end up someplace else ended up stuffed in a bell pepper. In terms of technique, since you do little more than warm these peppers in the oven, it's a good idea to parboil them before stuffing (which I find easier), or add a little water to the pan and cover it to make steam during cooking. If you have any of the sauce from Crawfish Etouffée (page 104) left over, pour about 2 ounces of it over each pepper and try serving this with some fried catfish on the side.

MELT the butter in a large pan and sauté the onions, celery, green peppers, and chicken livers over medium heat until the onions are translucent, about 5 minutes. Add the crawfish, seasoning, pepper, Tabasco, bay leaves, and chicken stock; increase the heat to high; and bring to a boil. Add the rice and boil, uncovered, for 3 minutes. Cover, turn off the heat, and allow the rice to steam in the pan until it is cooked, about 15 minutes.

Preheat the oven to 350 degrees.

Stir the green onions into the crawfish-rice stuffing. Remove and discard the bay leaves. Season the mixture to taste with salt, then stuff into the parboiled green peppers. Heat in the oven for 5 to 10 minutes in a deep baking pan with about ¹/₄ inch of water at the bottom of the pan. Serve hot on dinner plates.

NOTE: To parboil peppers, place cleaned peppers in a pot of lightly salted boiling water for 1 to 2 minutes. Remove them, then place them in a bath of ice and water until cooled. Drain and set aside.

Crawfish Picante

Serves 8

Some days in the kitchen, everybody ends up fantasizing about the same taste, and in my kitchen, that often means something Mexican. Maybe I never got over growing up next to New Orleans's first Mexican restaurant! Anyway, when this happens during crawfish season, at least one daily special is guaranteed to taste something like this.

HEAT the olive oil in a medium sauté pan over medium heat, add the garlic and tomato paste, and sauté 1 to 2 minutes. Add all of the remaining ingredients except the crawfish and rice and cook, reducing by half, about 5 minutes. Add the crawfish and cook just to heat thoroughly.

To serve, spoon over steamed white rice.

3 tablespoons olive oil

4 cloves garlic, chopped

1 tablespoon tomato paste

1 green bell pepper, seeded, deribbed, and julienned

1 red bell pepper, seeded, deribbed, and julienned

1 cup chicken stock (page 149)

2 tablespoons tequila

1/4 cup diced jalapeño peppers

4 cups tomato sauce

1/2 tablespoon chile powder

1/2 teaspoon ground cumin

1 pound crawfish tails, peeled

3 cups steamed white rice

Crawfish-Eggplant Casserole

2 eggplants, peeled and diced

1/4 cup butter

1 cup diced onions

1 cup diced celery

1 cup diced green bell peppers

1/4 cup chopped fresh parsley

6 cloves garlic, chopped

1 1/2 cups diced cooked chicken

1 1/2 cups peeled crawfish tails

1 tablespoon Italian seasoning (page 149)

1 tablespoon blackening seasoning (page 145)

1 1/2 cups chicken stock (page 149)

1 teaspoon Worcestershire sauce

1 teaspoon Crystal hot sauce or other Louisiana hot sauce

1/2 cup finely chopped green onions

1 cup Italian-style bread crumbs plus additional for sprinkling

1/2 cup freshly grated Parmesan cheese

Serves 6 to 8

My mother made this casserole all the time when I was growing up. It was a typical New Orleans–Sicilian way of working with what you had. For an extra treat, you can substitute anise-sweet Italian sausage for the chicken or just add a little to the mix in this recipe. If you want the taste, who's going to tell you no? Certainly not my mother.

TO prepare the eggplants, place them in a large pot of lightly salted boiling water and boil until tender, 3 to 5 minutes. Drain and set aside.

Melt the butter in a large pan over medium heat; add the onions, celery, green peppers, parsley, and garlic; and sauté until the onions are translucent, about 8 minutes. Add the remaining ingredients.

Preheat the oven to 350 degrees.

Transfer the eggplant mixture to a casserole dish and sprinkle with additional bread crumbs. Heat in the oven for 10 minutes, or until golden brown on top. Serve hot on dinner plates.

Louisiana Chowder

Serves 8

Sometimes in Louisiana, crawfish share top billing with other types of seafood, as they do in this terrific French-influenced chowder. For the fish, I especially like to use shark, one of those newly utilized (but, of course, very old) fish from the Gulf, or the deservedly popular amberjack.

MELT the butter in a large soup pot over medium heat; add the onions, celery, and green peppers; and sauté until the onions are translucent, about 7 minutes. Add the potatoes and stock and bring to a boil. Add the remaining ingredients except for the flour and water and return to a boil over medium heat.

In a bowl, dissolve the flour in the water; pour this mixture into the chowder. Adjust the heat to allow for a light boil or simmer. Cook until the liquid thickens, about 10 minutes. Serve in deep bowls.

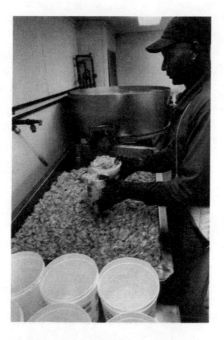

2 cups butter

1 cup diced onions

1 cup diced celery

1 cup diced green bell peppers

2 cups peeled, diced potatoes

2 quarts fish stock (page 148)

$^1/_2$ tablespoon freshly ground black pepper

$^1/_2$ teaspoon dried thyme

$^1/_4$ teaspoon freshly ground red pepper

2 tablespoons Worcestershire sauce

$^1/_4$ pound crawfish tail meat, peeled

$^1/_2$ pound boneless firm-fleshed fish (such as redfish, amberjack, or shark), cut into chunks

$^1/_4$ pound small (50 to 60 count) shrimp, peeled

$^1/_2$ cup oyster water

$^1/_4$ pound oyster meat

1 cup corn kernels

$^1/_4$ cup finely sliced green onions

$^1/_2$ cup all-purpose flour

1 cup cold water

Summer Crawfish and Pasta Salad

Serves 6

One summer day, I guess I was dreaming of a light, fresh pasta salad at the same time I was craving a little New Orleans–style Vietnamese food. Or maybe you have some better explanation of the hows and whys of this dish. Just trust me on the chile paste and the sesame oil, okay? If you don't trust me now, you certainly will after you taste this salad.

COMBINE ingredients for the salad in a bowl and refrigerate to chill for about 1 hour. In a small bowl, thoroughly mix together the dressing ingredients. Toss the chilled salad with the dressing.

To serve, divide the salad over beds of shredded lettuce on individual plates.

Salad

¹/₂ yellow bell pepper, seeded, deribbed, and julienned

¹/₂ red bell pepper, seeded, deribbed, and julienned

¹/₂ red onion, julienned

4 tablespoons finely chopped green onions

1 pound cooked crawfish tail meat, peeled

1 pound rotini, cooked and drained

Dressing

1 cup red wine vinegar

2 tablespoons sesame oil

1 teaspoon Asian chile paste

3 cups shredded iceberg lettuce

Marinated Crawfish Salad

Serves 4

You can't get much quicker or easier than this fresh and light salad for a long, hot summer. One trick is to use extra virgin olive oil instead of the cheaper not-so-virgin kind. Another trick is to turn the salad at least 50 times with your hands, a method that ensures covering every inch of everything with great taste—and it's just about marinated by the time you finish. (Your hands are marinated by this time too.)

I N a large bowl, hand-toss all of the ingredients except the lettuce until thoroughly combined—50 turns works well. Place in the refrigerator to marinate for 1 to 2 hours.

To serve, spoon the salad over beds of shredded lettuce on individual plates.

1 cup crawfish tail meat, peeled

1 tablespoon minced garlic

1/2 tablespoon blackening seasoning (page 145)

1 tablespoon finely chopped green onions

1/8 teaspoon salt

1/4 cup extra virgin olive oil

2 cups shredded iceberg lettuce

EVERYBODY who lives in New Orleans, and just about everybody who visits us here, knows about "lagniappe"—the local Creole tradition of "something extra." It's an old-fashioned French word, if you bother saying it right with the accent on the last syllable. Not too many of us think that's worth the effort, and instead just say "lan-yap" and hope the tourists can come close.

Lan-yap is close enough for government work. Especially government work in Louisiana, if you know what I mean.

As I see it, lagniappe is like a lot of things here in New Orleans: it's both simple and profound. In a simple way, it's the same little dose of customer relations implied in the phrase "baker's dozen." It's a straight case of "ya bought twelve eggs; here's one more on me."

This used to be so much easier, before all our groceries were scanned at the register and kept under close control by computers. Just here's a little bit extra; I won't tell the boss if you won't. This was the magical Creole exchange, even when the guy giving you the lagniappe was the boss.

As late as my childhood, though for the most part not anymore, the tradition of lagniappe formed and gave meaning to the transactions of our lives.

Despite the loss of day-to-day extras—the rice put in the bag for free when you bought your Monday red beans, the mustard greens thrown in when you bought your salty ham hock—lagniappe remains alive in New Orleans. In a way, perhaps we can see it even more clearly now, without the clutter of buying and selling. Lagniappe is a spirit of remarkable generosity, one that seldom grew here from wealth but flourished here in adversity.

For better or worse, if you want to find lagniappe of any kind today, go looking on the many poor sides of town. From shopkeepers who actually do as their grandparents did to untrained cooks who invite you to sample their mama's recipe to weak old people who give a uniformed private school student their seat on the bus "because he looked tired," I'm here to tell you lagniappe lives.

This chapter started out simply, as a small collection of non-seafood dishes that are so important we couldn't leave them out—even out of a seafood book. Then, once we got cooking (literally, in this case), we thought: Oh, what about all those side dishes, like maque choux (a Cajun smothered corn dish) or smothered greens or cornbread, that go so great with our seafood? Only later, as we wrestled to wrap these two gifts in one package, did we realize what we were dealing with was lagniappe all along.

So, a lot of these dishes are traditional. Most, in fact, no chef would dare monkey around with much. When people order red beans and rice in New Orleans, they're not lusting after a red bean–ancho chile frittata with white rice coulis. Trust me on this, okay? They want red beans and rice the way their mama or daddy or grandma or Aunt Suzie made it, and you had better cook it for them.

With a lot of allowances for a lot of variations, I've stayed in business all these years cooking these dishes these ways. It works in my kitchen. More importantly, it works in my dining room, both at the restaurant and at home. And it will work for you.

I believe you see lagniappe for real in the way we New Orleanians cook at home. Some people figure, I suppose, that we cook such big batches of things like gumbo and jambalaya so we can either eat till we pop or freeze individual leftovers for work. We do both those things. But the reason we cook so much is, quite simply, so we can have more to give away.

We love to invite friends and relatives over to eat. We love to ladle out still more for them to take home. And we love to just turn up at people's doors saying, "Hey, I made lots of my chicken and andouille gumbo. I think it'll knock your socks off." In this town, with our food, we never seem to keep our socks on.

Carnival Cornbread

Makes 9 squares

Even traditional cornbread gets fire in its eyes when jalapeño peppers are added. The green of these peppers joins the red bell peppers to make a confetti-colorful treat.

PREHEAT the oven to 400 degrees. Grease a 9-inch square pan and set aside. In a medium bowl, combine the flour, cornmeal, baking powder, and salt. In another medium bowl, lightly beat the eggs, then stir in the buttermilk, butter, and honey.

Form a well in the center of the dry ingredients, add the milk mixture all at once, and stir just enough to combine. Stir in the peppers. Spoon the batter into the greased pan and bake in the preheated oven for 20 minutes, or until a cake tester inserted in the center comes out clean.

Place on a wire rack. Cool 10 minutes, then cut into squares and remove from the pan. Serve warm.

1 cup all-purpose flour

1 cup yellow cornmeal

1 tablespoon baking powder

$\frac{1}{2}$ teaspoon salt

2 large eggs

1 cup buttermilk

$\frac{1}{4}$ cup butter, melted

2 tablespoons honey

1 jalapeño pepper, minced

1 cup minced red bell peppers

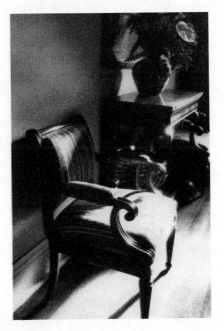

Oyster Dressing

1 loaf stale French bread, cubed

About 1 quart water

3 tablespoons butter

1/2 cup chopped green bell peppers

1/2 cup chopped celery

1/2 cup chopped onions

24 oysters, shucked

1 cup oyster water

1 teaspoon Tabasco sauce

1 teaspoon coarsely ground black pepper

1/2 teaspoon Worcestershire sauce

1 teaspoon salt

1/3 cup toasted pecan pieces

1/3 cup chopped green onions

Serves 6

In other parts of the South people rely on cornbread to stuff or serve with a holiday turkey, but most of us here in New Orleans prefer an oyster dressing. Every true New Orleans cook makes an oyster dressing he or she is convinced puts every other one to shame. This stovetop version is our favorite, at holiday or anytime. Serve the stuffing with any type of fresh fish, or try it alongside poultry, beef, or pork.

PUT the bread in a large bowl and cover with the water. Remove as much water as possible by pressing through a colander with your hands.

Melt the butter in a large sauté pan over medium heat. Add the green peppers, celery, and onions and sauté until translucent, 4 to 5 minutes. Add 2 cups of the bread, the oysters, oyster water, Tabasco, black pepper, Worcestershire sauce, and salt and cook over high heat until reduced by half, or until the dressing holds its shape. Sprinkle the pecan pieces and green onions over the top, and serve in a large bowl.

Soul Food Okra and Shrimp

Serves 6

As classy a set of flavors as this recipe produces, I like to remember that shrimp and okra are a New Orleans soul food staple. But even if you didn't hear that from me, you might guess it from the glorious simplicity of putting all of these ingredients in one big pot and cooking them until they get super-friendly. You can ladle the rich stew that develops over steamed white rice or enjoy it all by itself.

COMBINE all of the ingredients except the shrimp in a large soup pot. Bring to a boil over medium heat and then reduce the heat and simmer, covered, for 1 1/2 hours. Add the shrimp and cook for 20 minutes more. Serve hot.

1/2 cup butter

2 cups chopped onions

2 cups chopped green bell peppers

2 cups chopped celery

1/4 cup chopped garlic

1/2 cup chopped fresh parsley

1/2 cup chopped green onions

1-pound package frozen okra (defrosted)

4 1/2 teaspoons salt

1 tablespoon freshly ground black pepper

2 bay leaves

1 tablespoon dried thyme

1 1/2 teaspoons dried basil

1 16-ounce can (2 cups) crushed tomatoes

1/2 tablespoon blackening seasoning (page 145)

2 tablespoons Crystal hot sauce or other Louisiana hot sauce

1 1/2 pounds small (50 to 60 count) shrimp, peeled

Garlic Pasta

Serves 4

3 cups garlic butter (page 146)

2 pounds linguine, cooked and drained

2 tablespoons chopped green onions

Salt

3 tablespoons cracked black pepper

¾ cup pecorino-romano cheese

Here's a delicious way to use our garlic butter (page 146). You can serve this pasta as a savory side dish to many of the seafood entrées in this book or top it with three or four grilled shrimp and serve it as an entrée.

MELT the garlic butter in a large pan over medium heat. Add the pasta and toss to cover and heat through. Sprinkle with the green onions and season with the salt and pepper. Divide onto plates, sprinkle with the cheese, and serve.

Maque Choux

Serves 10 to 12

16 ears fresh corn

1 tablespoon unsalted butter

1 tablespoon vegetable oil

1 cup chopped onions

1 cup chopped green bell peppers

1 teaspoon freshly ground white pepper

½ teaspoon ground red pepper

½ teaspoon dried thyme

2 cups chopped tomatoes

Salt

3 tablespoons heavy whipping cream

This dish is one the French learned from the Native Americans who lived in south Louisiana long before Europeans arrived. The name is a French phonetic spelling of the dish's Indian name.

USING a sharp knife, cut the kernels from the ears, scraping the ears to obtain the milky pulp. You should have about 8 cups of kernels. In a skillet, heat the butter and oil and add the onions and green peppers. Cook until soft, about 3 minutes. Add the corn, white and red pepper, and thyme, and cook until the corn starts to stick to the bottom of the pan, about 10 minutes. Add the tomatoes, salt, and cream and cook, stirring regularly, until thick, about 10 minutes. Serve hot.

Smothered Greens

Serves 10

Any city dweller should learn how to make a meal out of collard, mustard, turnip, or other greens. And whatever you do, don't toss out the cooking liquid, known as "pot likker"—you can sip that like soup between bites of cornbread.

COOK the bacon in a heavy kettle over medium heat until the fat is rendered, about 10 minutes. Add the onions, celery, and red peppers and cook, stirring constantly, over medium heat for about 5 minutes. Add the greens, cover, and cook until the greens are wilted, about 15 minutes. Add the ham hocks, salt and pepper to taste, and vinegar to the pan; cover; and cook for another 15 minutes. Pour in the water, cover, and simmer for 90 minutes, stirring occasionally. Serve in individual bowls.

NOTE: Try serving this over rice as a side for Fried Catfish (page 94).

3/4 cup lean bacon, cut in cubes

1 cup finely chopped onions

1/2 cup chopped celery

3/4 cup chopped red bell peppers

7 pounds greens (collard, mustard, turnip, or other greens, or a combination of greens), torn into 2-inch pieces

2 (1/4-pound) ham hocks

Salt and black pepper

2 tablespoons white wine vinegar

2 cups water

Red Beans and Rice

1 pound kidney beans

8 cups water

1 cup chopped onions

1 pound pickled pork or ham, cut in cubes

1 bay leaf

2 tablespoons minced garlic

2 sprigs parsley, chopped

Salt and black pepper

4 cups steamed white rice

1 pound andouille or other smoked sausage, cut into strips

Serves 6

Times have changed since the days when Monday existed for putting on a big pot of red beans and doing the week's laundry. But red beans tend to be on that day's menus in even the fanciest restaurants in New Orleans.

RINSE the beans in cold water, put them in a medium bowl, add water to cover, and soak the beans overnight.

Drain the beans and transfer them to a large pot. Add the water and simmer, uncovered, for 1 hour over low heat. Add the onions and pork and cook until tender, about 50 minutes. Add the bay leaf, garlic, and parsley and season to taste with salt and pepper. Cook for about 30 minutes more, until the beans start to become creamy.

Serve over white rice with strips of smoked andouille sausage on the side.

NOTE: To ensure a creamy texture, mash some of the beans with a potato masher.

Chicken and Andouille Gumbo

Serves 8 to 10

While seafood remains the culinary coin of our realm, this country gumbo says a mouthful, too. It proves that in Louisiana, old cooking ideas never die, they just find new ingredients to showcase. The optional filé powder is ground sassafras leaves, a final sprinkle taught to the early Creoles by the Native Americans who lived north of Lake Pontchartrain.

BROWN the sausage on both sides in a large pan over medium-high heat and set aside. Make a roux by combining the margarine with the flour in the pan along with the sausage drippings, stirring constantly over medium heat until the flour is a medium brown, about 10 minutes. Add the onions and celery and cook, stirring, just until translucent, about 5 minutes. Add all of the remaining ingredients plus the reserved sausage and cook until the flavors blend, 25 to 30 minutes. Serve hot.

2 pounds andouille or other smoked sausage, sliced into discs

4 cups margarine or butter

4 cups all-purpose flour

4 cups diced onions

4 cups diced celery

2 cups dry sherry

4 large bay leaves, crushed

3 pounds chicken, diced

5 tablespoons hot pepper sauce

1 tablespoon ground black pepper

5 tablespoons Worcestershire sauce

1 tablespoon ground red pepper

8 quarts chicken stock (page 149)

2 tablespoons salt

4 tablespoons filé powder (optional)

Jambalaya

Serves 8 to 10

1/4 pound margarine

3 cups chopped onions

3 cups chopped celery

3 cups chopped green
bell peppers

1 pound small (50 to 60
count) raw shrimp,
peeled

1 pound chicken breast,
boned, skinned, and
cut into bite-size
cubes

1 pound andouille or
other smoked
sausage, sliced into
discs

3 teaspoons black
pepper

3 teaspoons blackening
seasoning (page 145)

3 tablespoons hot pep-
per sauce

3 bay leaves

4 cups crushed canned
tomatoes, with juice

2 quarts chicken stock
(page 149)

2 pounds white rice

Besides providing Hank Williams with a title for one of his most famous songs, jambalaya provides New Orleanians with a basic recipe into which they can toss virtually anything in the refrigerator. Here's one of our favorite versions.

MELT the margarine and sauté the onions, celery, and peppers over medium heat until translucent, about 5 minutes. Stir in the shrimp, chicken, and sausage, sautéing until the chicken is cooked, 5 to 7 minutes. Add all of the remaining ingredients except the rice and bring to a boil. Add the rice and cover the pot with a tight-fitting lid. Bring to a boil again, and then turn off the heat and allow the stew to sit until the rice absorbs all of the liquid, about 20 minutes. Fluff the stew with a fork and serve hot in individual bowls.

Tomato Basil Pasta

Serves 4

Don't be stingy with the cheese on this one.

IN a medium saucepan, sauté the olive oil and garlic over medium heat, about 3 minutes. Add the marsala and stir to deglaze the pan, scraping browned bits from the bottom. Add the canned and fresh tomatoes and the basil leaves and sauté until the sauce is reduced, 3 to 4 minutes. Add the garlic butter and remove the pan from the heat. Add the pasta and season to taste with the salt and black pepper. Toss just to heat the pasta. Sprinkle the cheese over the top, toss again, and serve.

1/4 cup extra virgin olive oil

3 teaspoons minced garlic

1/4 cup marsala

3 cups canned whole tomatoes, crushed by hand, with juice

1 1/4 cups chopped fresh tomatoes

10 fresh basil leaves

1 cup garlic butter (page 146)

2 pounds cooked linguine or other pasta

Salt and coarsely ground black pepper

2 cups freshly grated pecorino-romano cheese

I didn't grow up knowing and loving a lot of desserts. In a family that made its living from seafood, sweet finales took a back seat to just about everything else. This is not to say that none of us had a sweet tooth, but it did mean that some combination of fresh fruit and sugary snacks filled in where other people might have enjoyed a rotation through cakes and pies.

Popular New Orleans desserts are built around the bright yellow bunches of bananas that appear at our riverfront from the jungles of Central America. Not surprisingly, bananas are the star of my favorite dessert memory—though you can be sure Mr. Frank's "famous" Banana Fritters (page 141) are far removed from Bananas Foster flamed at tableside by a guy in a tuxedo. No, Mr. Frank was an Irishman, one of the people who turned up to work at the restaurant whenever times were hard. He and my father were fishing and drinking buddies, which meant weeks at a time spent at our fishing camp—my dad, Mr. Frank, my brother, and me. The camp was a house built on stilts in the water, and we escaped there in the summer to get away from the heat of the city and also to fish, crab, shrimp, trap, hunt, and just have a party. Mr. Frank served as camp cook. Sometimes for dessert, and often for breakfast, he'd whip up his incredible banana fritters.

But there's more to this memory than fritters. My dad, always looking for a deal, rarely bought those puny bunches of bananas sold at the grocery store. Instead, he'd wander down to the riverfront to the banana docks and bargain with the guys there for a cutting as big as a tree. And a tree was what these bananas looked like to me, especially when my dad hung them from the ceiling in the middle of the camp. Whether it was Mr. Frank picking bananas for fritters or me just grabbing a banana for a sandwich on French bread with butter, having our own bananas "growing" indoors was as much dessert as I needed more days than not.

There were only a couple of traditional exceptions to our family's limited sweets menu. One was any time my Sicilian relatives got involved, especially around St. Joseph's Day. All over New Orleans, for that feast in March devoted to the patron saint of Sicily, there were altars of food pulled together by women who cooked for days and days. That meant Sicilian desserts like spumoni (which I've loved all my life) and cannoli (which most people loved more than I did) are a regular part of New Orleans life. (To me, there isn't much that is more New Orleans than the way Sicilians celebrate St. Joseph and the Irish celebrate St. Patrick at virtually the same time. Just picture it: two sets of Catholics eating and drinking too much, in honor of two statues smiling down on the party!)

The other dessert I grew up with was seasonal, when the strawberries reached New Orleans from Ponchatoula across Lake Pontchartrain. I've never tasted a better, sweeter, more perfect strawberry. For a brief period, they are everywhere. Shortcake is served around the clock, along with strawberry cakes and pies of every shape and size. My all-time favorite, though, is simple strawberries and cream—just pour some cream over a bowl of strawberries and sprinkle a little sugar on top.

At my restaurant today, we serve quite a few terrific desserts, several of which I share with you here. To me, they put the "sweet" in the sweet life we live here in New Orleans.

Sweet Potato Orange Pie

Makes 2 pies

Sweet potato recipes remind us of how much New Orleans has learned about cooking from the slaves and the free people of color who lived and died here. Often mistakenly called yams, the dark orange sweet potatoes are African through and through. Many of their uses were developed by George Washington Carver. He apparently did sweet potatoes in his spare time, when he wasn't playing around with peanuts.

TO prepare the pie crust, stir together the flour and salt in a medium bowl. Add the oil and cold water and stir until a ball forms. Remove the ball from the bowl and cut in half with a sharp knife. Roll the halves out on a floured board to form two 12-inch circles.

Preheat the oven to 325 degrees.

To prepare the filling, boil the sweet potatoes until they are tender enough to mash. Drain them in a colander, transfer to a large bowl, and mash with a potato masher. Add the remaining ingredients for the filling. Press the dough into two 9-inch round pie pans, trim excess dough, and flute the edges with your thumb and index finger. Pour the mixture into the 2 pie shells. Bake in the oven for 25 minutes, or until a toothpick inserted in the center of the pies comes out clean. Cool to room temperature.

To make the topping, whip the cream with a whisk with the Grand Marnier and sugar until the mixture is stiff. Add a dollop of cream to each slice of pie.

Crust

2 cups all-purpose flour

1 1/2 teaspoons salt

1/2 cup vegetable oil

5 tablespoons cold water

Filling

2 pounds sweet potatoes, peeled and sliced

1/4 teaspoon ground cinnamon

1/4 teaspoon ground allspice

2 tablespoons orange zest, grated

Pinch of salt

1 1/3 cups sugar

1/3 cup freshly squeezed orange juice

4 eggs, lightly beaten

1 1/2 cups heavy whipping cream

Topping

2 cups heavy whipping cream

2 tablespoons Grand Marnier

1/2 cup confectioners' sugar

Strawberry Nonsense

Serves 8

4 teaspoons unflavored gelatin

2¹/₃ cups milk

²/₃ cup heavy whipping cream

1 tablespoon sugar

Zest of 2 lemons, grated

1 medium pound cake or sponge cake

1¹/₂ cups strawberries, hulled and quartered

¹/₃ cup sugar

Lemon Curd

1 cup freshly squeezed lemon juice

1 tablespoon grated lemon zest

²/₃ cup sugar

²/₃ cup butter

8 egg yolks

4 teaspoons unflavored gelatin

1 teaspoon vanilla extract

When the strawberries come in from Ponchatoula, you won't catch us building desserts around much of anything else. Guests at my restaurant love the way this slightly fancy dessert marries strawberries and lemon curd.

T O prepare the gelatin, place the gelatin in a medium saucepan and sprinkle ¹/₃ cup milk over it. Heat the mixture over medium-high heat just until boiling. Add the remaining 2 cups milk, the cream, sugar, and lemon zest. Remove the pan from the heat, cover it, and allow to steep for up to 30 minutes.

To prepare the bread, remove the crust from the pound cake using a sharp knife. Cut the cake into 1¹/₂-inch-thick slices and dry for 15 minutes in a 300-degree oven.

To prepare the strawberries, place them in a medium bowl and toss with the sugar. Set aside, reserving any syrup.

To prepare the lemon curd, combine the lemon juice and zest with the sugar and butter in the top of a double boiler. Place the pan over medium heat and cook until the sugar is dissolved, about 10 minutes. In a separate bowl, temper yolks with some of the lemon mixture. Combine this with the remaining lemon mixture in the double boiler, whisking until the mixture thickens. Strain and then reheat the milk mixture in a large pan over medium heat until simmering, about 5 minutes. Remove from the heat and stir in the gelatin and vanilla. Stir until gelatin is dissolved. Set aside and allow to cool.

To assemble, place a few cubes of the cake in the bottom of 8 custard cups. Pour enough of the milk mixture into the cups to cover. Add a layer of the berries with syrup and top off with more of the milk mixture. Refrigerate until set, about 45 minutes.

Remove the custards from the refrigerator and unmold by setting the cup in a shallow pan of hot water. Invert onto individual plates.

Coconut Cream Pie

Serves 8

Here's a pie that reminds me of my childhood, and probably will remind you of yours, too. It isn't that such pies were what we'd call "decadent" today, as much as that they were carefree. I'm not telling you that you shouldn't count fat grams if that's your idea of a great time. I am telling you that most people seemed a lot happier before we figured out how to do it.

PREHEAT the oven to 425 degrees.

To prepare the crust, combine the graham cracker crumbs and sugar in a medium bowl. Add the melted butter and stir to thoroughly combine. Press the mixture into a 10-inch pie pan, covering the sides of the pan first and then spreading evenly over the bottom of the pan. Bake in the oven for 8 minutes or until golden brown. Remove from the oven and place on a rack to cool.

To prepare the filling, pour ¹/₂ cup milk into a small bowl and sprinkle the gelatin over the top. Set aside to allow gelatin to soften. In a medium saucepan, combine the remaining 4 cups milk, butter, ¹/₂ cup of the sugar, and the salt. Measure 2 tablespoons of the coconut and set aside for garnish. Add the remaining coconut to the pan with the milk mixture and bring to a boil over medium heat.

Meanwhile, combine the remaining sugar and the cornstarch. Blend until smooth. Add the eggs and yolks, stirring to combine thoroughly.

When the coconut-milk mixture reaches a boil, add a small amount of the milk to the egg mixture to temper the eggs. Add the egg mixture to the saucepan with the milk-coconut mixture and cook over low heat until the mixture is thickened and bubbly, about 10 minutes. Remove the pan from the heat and pour the mixture into a large bowl. Cover and let cool for 10 minutes.

In a separate bowl, whip the cream until stiff peaks form. Fold the whipped cream into the coconut mixture. Pour the filling into the graham cracker crust, mounding it high in the center. Refrigerate for at least 1 hour to chill.

Crust

1¹/₂ cups graham cracker crumbs

¹/₂ cup granulated sugar

¹/₃ cup melted unsalted butter

Coconut Filling

4¹/₂ cups whole milk

1 tablespoon unflavored gelatin

3 tablespoons unsalted butter

³/₄ cup granulated sugar

Pinch of salt (optional)

2 cups flaked unsweetened coconut

¹/₃ cup cornstarch

2 eggs

4 egg yolks

1 cup heavy whipping cream

Topping

3 cups heavy whipping cream

3 tablespoons confectioners' sugar

continued from page 139

To prepare the topping, whip the cream for the topping with the confectioners' sugar until stiff peaks form. Fill a pastry bag fitted with the star tip with some of the whipped cream. Remove the pie from the refrigerator and cut it in half. Cut each half into 4 even slices. Pipe graceful spirals of the topping on each slice, starting from the edge of the pie pan and working toward the center, being careful not to obscure the cuts in the pie. Sprinkle the pie with the reserved coconut, and serve.

Bread Pudding

Serves 8

New Orleanians rank restaurants according to how well they like the bread pudding. That's not to say that any two local diners or cooks agree on what good bread pudding is; it's just that we all care plenty about the stuff. As a lot of my dad's buddies used to say, "That's what makes horse races." And based on the way they looked, whether rich or dead broke after a day at the fairgrounds, it's a safe bet these guys knew a horse race when they saw one.

1 loaf stale French bread, broken up

1 cup sugar

$1/2$ teaspoon salt

1 (8-ounce) can fruit cocktail, with juice

$1/2$ teaspoon vanilla extract

1 cup raisins

2 tablespoons unsalted butter, melted

1 quart milk

Whiskey Sauce

1 tablespoon bourbon

$1/4$ pound butter

$1 1/2$ cups sugar

$1 1/2$ cups heavy whipping cream

$3/4$ teaspoon ground nutmeg

$1/4$ teaspoon vanilla extract

PREHEAT the oven to 350 degrees.

Combine all of the ingredients for the pudding in a large bowl. Pour the mixture into a large greased baking dish and bake for 35 to 40 minutes, or until set.

When ready to serve, mix together all of the ingredients for the sauce in a medium saucepan and cook over medium-high heat until the volume is reduced by about half, about 5 minutes. Spoon the sauce over individual servings of the bread pudding, about 2 ounces each. Serve immediately.

Pecan Pie

Serves 10 to 12

*There aren't too many ways that New Orleans is a Southern city—
we're just too European, even Mediterranean, for that. But if we had
to let one notion in from the rest of the South, we could have done
lots worse than pecan pie. Besides, with all the pecans we grow and
all the sugarcane we harvest, we probably never had a choice.*

PREHEAT the oven to 350 degrees.

Sift together the sugar and salt in a medium bowl, and beat
in the eggs, melted butter, cream, Karo syrup, and vanilla. Stir in
the pecans and pour the mixture into the pie shells. Bake until set,
about 25 minutes. Allow to cool and slice to serve.

2 cups sugar

1/2 teaspoon salt

6 eggs

1 1/2 tablespoons butter,
melted

3/4 cup heavy whipping
cream

3/4 cup dark Karo brand
syrup

1/2 teaspoon vanilla
extract

2 cups chopped pecans

2 unbaked 10-inch pie
crusts (page 150)

Mr. Frank's Banana Fritters

Serves 6

*Mr. Frank's banana fritters come out like the air-light fried French
doughnuts called beignets served with powdered sugar in shops near
the French Market, but this recipe is for the fritters Mr. Frank fixed
all the time at our fishing camp. He would pick ripe bananas from
the huge stalk my Dad kept hanging inside the camp whenever he
could get a great price down at the docks. For breakfast or dessert, if
you ask me, it doesn't get any better than this.*

IN a medium bowl, beat the egg with the milk and oil with a
whisk. Stir in the sugar, baking powder, baking soda, and salt. Slice
the bananas and stir them into the batter. Deep-fry the battered
banana slices in batches in a fryer in oil preheated to 350 degrees
until golden brown, 3 to 4 minutes. Drain on paper towels, sprinkle with the confectioners' sugar, and serve hot.

1 egg

1 1/4 cups milk

2 tablespoons oil

2 tablespoons sugar

2 teaspoons baking
powder

1/2 teaspoon baking soda

1/2 teaspoon salt

3 ripe bananas

Vegetable oil for deep-
frying

Confectioners' sugar for
dusting

BUILDING blocks. That's what this entire book has been about, in case you hadn't noticed. And that's what I'm about, as a New Orleans chef who grew up around every possible type of New Orleans cook. What I've given you in these pages are building blocks.

Since this is the final chapter, I can admit this to you. The hardest part about writing this book was learning to rethink the food of my life into finished recipes. I know that's what so many of you want from a cookbook, a one-stop shop that will knock 'em dead at dinnertime, with every little up and down of perfect procedure.

I hope you agree by this point that we have given you that. But I can assure you: that's not how we think here.

In any traditional New Orleans kitchen, and I mean homes, not restaurants, there's actually no such thing as a finished dish. The only finished dish in my mama's kitchen was a dish that was all gone, which is precisely how all of her dishes ended up. Otherwise, it was the bright red Sicilian stew that got a quick hit of heavy cream and became a pasta sauce. Otherwise, it was the last remaining fried soft-shell that took on new life (not to mention lettuce and tomato) as the world's best po-boy.

You see, in my mama's kitchen, as eventually in my daddy's restaurant and now in mine, everything we do is a building block. The result is not a menu of finished dishes (though that's what you think you're getting when you order dinner) but a twenty-four-hour-a-day, seven-day-a-week process built on the crazy-committed love of flavor.

What follows in this chapter is, I hope, every elemental component you'll need to cook my food the way I cook it. These recipes work because they are age-old basics, the way good bones beget good stocks beget good sauces beget good dishes, especially when the dishes form around fabulous seafood and produce, with just the right kick from spice. There's more begetting in a New Orleans kitchen than you'll find in the Bible.

Before I let you go off into your own kitchen, let me plead with you as I've done nowhere else. Do not consider any one of these recipes the end of the line. They are only the beginning of an adventure you yourself will lead. I can take you only so far into the heart and soul of New Orleans. Beyond this point, you have to make this place and these people and this food your own.

Know that I'm cheering you on. Know that I'm here in case you get in a jam. And know that when you make too much of something (the way we always do in New Orleans), you can always invite me over. It's all about food and wine, all about passion, and all about people.

Sometimes visitors tell me about bread recipes from all around this country that use the same yeast mixtures again and again. They talk about the starter in sourdough or the wet, bubbling birthplace of "friendship bread," and they think the process is so unique. Of course I pretend to agree with them. But I always catch myself thinking: here in New Orleans, everything we cook is just like that. It has a life of its own. It goes on and on, even longer than we do.

I've invited you into not just my restaurant but also my family because I think you'll learn about my hometown there. How we live. How we see things. How we get through the day, with our own special blend of frustration and joy tipping toward celebration. This is us, and if you enter these recipes the way I hope you will, we will never be strangers again.

Do this for me. When you go to bed tonight, set aside for some bizarre version of the tooth fairy any thoughts that food is ever finished, any more than our food adventure is ever finished. Wake up tomorrow knowing that everything you cooked before is a building block for everything you cook from now on. If you do that, you'll wake up not just thinking the way we think—but living the way we live.

Blackening Seasoning

Makes about 1 cup

This spice blend gets its name from its use in "blackening" seafood or meat over very high heat in Cajun restaurants. It's our all-purpose Creole/Cajun spice blend. We recommend it highly over the commercial mixes available in grocery stores.

PLACE all of the spices in a bowl and mix together with a whisk. The seasoning can be stored about 1 week in an airtight container.

5 tablespoons paprika

1 tablespoon ground black pepper

1 tablespoon ground red pepper

1 tablespoon ground white pepper

1 tablespoon dried thyme, crushed with a mortar and pestle

2 tablespoons garlic powder

1 tablespoon powdered oregano

1 teaspoon salt

1 teaspoon chile powder

1 teaspoon onion powder

Seasoned Flour

Makes 1¹/₂ cups

We use this basic mixture in any savory dish calling for flour.

TO prepare the seasoned flour, mix together all of the ingredients in a large bowl.

1 cup all-purpose flour

1 teaspoon freshly ground red pepper

2 teaspoons salt

2 teaspoons freshly ground black pepper

1 teaspoon garlic powder

Cocktail Sauce

2 cups ketchup

1 tablespoon freshly
squeezed lemon juice

1 tablespoon
Worcestershire sauce

1¹/₂ tablespoons pre-
pared horseradish

¹/₈ teaspoon chile powder

Makes 2¹/₂ cups

This homemade sauce far outshines any available in grocery stores. You can add heat with a dash of pepper sauce if the horseradish isn't kick enough.

MIX together all of the ingredients in a medium bowl. Serve with any type of boiled seafood.

Garlic Butter

2 pounds butter, at room
temperature

1¹/₂ cups chopped fresh
parsley

¹/₂ cup romano cheese

1¹/₂ cups minced garlic

¹/₂ cup garlic powder

1¹/₂ cups chopped green
onions

Makes 8 cups

There's almost no limit to the uses of this wonderful sauce/condiment/coating. For proof, just spoon a little of this over the next sizzling steak you take off the grill.

PLACE the butter in a mixing bowl. Add all of the remaining ingredients and mix at low speed with a handheld mixer for 1 to 2 minutes. Then mix on high speed for 2 minutes or until fluffy. Cover with plastic wrap and store in the refrigerator for up to a week.

NOTE: Garlic butter has about a million uses. You can use it anywhere that butter is used for additional flavor (except maybe baking). Try serving it as a spread on any hot bread.

If you don't want this much, just reduce the recipe by half. But trust me, make the big batch and you'll find you can't do without it.

Brandy Cream Sauce

Makes 3 cups

I designed this sauce to use with shrimp, but, in truth, I haven't found anything in my kitchen this sauce doesn't make better. It's one of those rare sauces that's as good with meat as it is with seafood.

I N a medium saucepan over medium-high heat, melt the butter and add the blackening seasoning. Cook for 2 to 3 minutes. Briefly remove the pan from the heat as you add the brandy. Return it to the heat and cook until the brandy is almost gone, about 1 minute. Add the whipping cream and bring to a boil. Stir and reduce by half, or until the mixture is thick enough to coat the back of a spoon, about 5 minutes. Stir in the green onions.

$1/4$ cup butter

4 tablespoons blackening seasoning (page 145)

$1/3$ cup brandy

4 cups heavy whipping cream

$1/4$ cup finely chopped green onions

Creamy Crab Sauce

Makes $3/4$ cup

To take our garlic butter (page 146) to the next level, use this recipe for a flavorful topping. It is a delicious upgrade for just about any kind of seafood and also works well with poulty and beef.

I N a small sauté pan, stir the garlic butter over medium heat just until hot, then add the crabmeat and green onions. Stir gently to avoid shredding the crabmeat. Serve hot over prepared seafood.

$1/2$ cup garlic butter (page 146)

$1/4$ cup crabmeat, picked clean of any shell fragments

1 tablespoon thinly sliced green onions

Fish Stock

Makes 2¹/₂ quarts

3 quarts water

1 pound fish bones, cleaned

¹/₂ cup chopped shallots

¹/₂ leek, chopped

¹/₂ cup chopped celery

¹/₂ cup chopped fresh parsley

Pinch of dried thyme

1 bay leaf

3 black peppercorns

¹/₂ cup white wine

Just about any seafood dish is helped along by the addition of a full-flavored seafood stock, whether this traditional one made from fish or a dozen variations on the theme, mixing in shellfish, such as shrimp, crabs, or crawfish, to achieve a specific taste.

P L A C E all of the ingredients in a stockpot and bring to a boil over medium-high heat. Reduce the heat to low and simmer for 15 minutes. Remove the pan from the heat, skim away the froth, and strain the liquid through a wire-mesh strainer. Use immediately or place in a tightly covered container and refrigerate until ready to use, for up to 3 days. It can also be frozen.

Basic Whitewash

Makes 2¹/₂ cups

1 cup all-purpose flour

2 cups water

Whitewash is used in soups and stews as a thickening agent. For best results, remove about 2 cups of the liquid you are cooking to a small mixing bowl. In a slow, steady stream, whisk in the desired amount of whitewash. Once incorporated, pour the new mixture back into the main pot.

C O M B I N E the ingredients in a mixing bowl and whisk them together until they are smooth and incorporated.

Chicken Stock

Makes 4 quarts

Chicken stock is one of the most useful ingredients for any cook. The Creoles would never have gone without it, since a ladleful did things to recipes you would never expect and would hate to miss.

PREHEAT the oven to 400 degrees. Place the bones in a roasting pan and brown them in the oven for 15 to 20 minutes.

Bring the water to a boil over high heat in a large stockpot. Add the browned bones and the remaining ingredients, reduce the heat to medium, and simmer for 1 hour, or until the liquid is reduced by half. Remove the pan from the heat and allow the stock to cool, then refrigerate.

Remove all of the fat that has gathered at the surface of the liquid, then strain the stock with a colander. Refrigerate in a sealed plastic container until ready to use, for up to 3 days, or freeze.

2 pounds chicken bones

8 quarts water

1 cup peeled and chopped carrots

1/2 cup chopped onions

1/2 cup chopped celery, with leaves

1/2 cup chopped fresh parsley

Pinch of fresh thyme leaves

1 bay leaf

Salt and ground white pepper

Italian Seasoning

Makes 1/4 cup

While not as multi-purpose as the Creole or Cajun seasoning we call blackening seasoning, this blend will make most things taste better.

MIX together all the herbs and store in an airtight jar. Simple, eh??

1 tablespoon dried basil

1 tablespoon dried thyme

1 tablespoon dried oregano

2 teaspoons dried rosemary

Pie Crust

½ cup shortening

1½ cups all-purpose flour

2 tablespoons water

Makes one 10-inch pie crust

Like every other region of the Deep South, New Orleans loves pie. This recipe works with desserts, of course, but it is also good with several savory variations involving seafood.

IN a medium bowl, mix the shortening and the flour with a spoon, then add the water. Mix, cover the bowl, and let the mixture stand at room temperature for 30 minutes. Roll out the dough and place in a 10-inch pie plate.

INDEX

ABOUT THE AUTHORS

CHEF ANDREW JAEGER grew up over the New Orleans seafood restaurant his family ran for 45 years. Working his way through every job in the house, Chef Andrew eventually went out on his own, experimenting with a number of culinary concepts before finding tremendous success with Andrew Jaeger's House of Seafood in the French Quarter.

photo by Michael Palumbo

JOHN DEMERS is a New Orleans native who still lives in his hometown after eating his way through more than 100 foreign countries as UPI's globetrotting food editor. His food and wine commentaries are fixtures on New Orleans television and radio. This is his seventeenth book.

photo by Rhonda Findley